NEW SUBWAYS
A BUSINESS SOLUTION

By

JOSEPH C. FREEHOFF

ARTES
VERITAS
SCIENTIA
LIBRARY OF THE
UNIVERSITY OF MICHIGAN
TUEBOR
TRANSPORTATION
LIBRARY

NEW SUBWAYS
A Business Solution

An analysis showing that five cents covers the actual and necessary cost of carrying a passenger on new and existing rapid transit lines merged into a unified system wherein trunk and feeder line tracks bear such a proportion to each other that both can be operated with a minimum of idleness of track and waste in the movement of cars.

By
JOSEPH C. FREEHOFF, Ph.D.
Statistician with the Public Service Commission, State of New York, 1908-1921; formerly Professor of Economics, Cornell College. Author of The Panama Canal Tolls Controversy, Nature and Value of Money, and America and the Canal Title.

Trade Selling Agents
THE BAKER & TAYLOR CO.
55 Fifth Ave. NEW YORK At 12th St.

Bound by
J. F. TAPLEY CO.
Long Island City
N. Y.

PREFACE

We did not essay the role of critic. Events of the last seven, twelve or twenty-five years are not re-hashed. We describe and analyze the transit situation as it is today in order to place before the reader the facts necessary for judgment as to what can and should be done to expedite the construction of the additional transit facilities to relieve congestion and provide accommodation for the annual increase in traffic without retarding the erection of the urgently needed school buildings. That which stands athwart progress in these directions is mirrored and the conclusion to which the facts point are presented to the public for judgment.

Faultfinding leads nowhere. It irritates and, in so doing, prevents understanding through compromise. Criticism of past performance or non-performance does not hasten construction of new subways or the lengthening of station platforms on existing subways. We meerly point the way to a solution demanded by the economics and justified by the ethics of the situation.

Carrying passengers is a business enterprise. At the pre-war price level it was profitable at a five-cent fare. As a result of the upheaval in the price level due to forces set in motion by the World War a passenger cannot now be carried for five cents on the rapid transit lines and cover costs unless items now included in costs are either reduced or excluded through modification of the existing legal structure, and the theory underlying planning of new lines. Either revenue must be increased through a higher fare or costs must be reduced through exclusion or reduction of items charged to income.

On the threshold of analysis we find that the operating companies of the rapid transit lines and the city are copartners. This relationship is based on a series of contracts. The upheaval in the price level due to the World War has made vital financial clauses in these contracts either obsolete or unworkable. Ordinary business insight shows that the financial clauses in these contracts should be revamped or should be superseded.

Modification of the financial clauses of the existing contracts so that the intent of the negotiators would be realized would be just, reasonable and conscionable. In-so-far as it could not be settled by negotiation resort to arbitration would be in order. But it is politically impossible. The five-cent fare is a political necessity. In this study, the writer shows how costs can be reduced through modification of the legal structure so that a five-cent fare will be adequate and the companies be compensated in the amount determined by the actuarial value of the earnings available for interest and dividend payment on the securities of the companies under the preferential system of revenue distribution in their contracts with the City.

In this analysis the writer shows that a passenger can be carried for five cents if a business service is rendered and that that is the way of approach to the problem if a solution is sought that is fair to the travelling public and to the companies. Charges that are not an actual and necessary part of the cost of carrying a passenger should be eliminated and thereafter a service that costs five cents should be the aim in the planning of new lines.

The transit problem is now largely a matter of municipal credit, that is, of debt-incurring power. Whence the money with which to construct new lines and purchase the equipment? It can be made available by increasing revenue through a higher fare or by reducing costs through modification of the existing legal structure. Another method is that proposed by Comptroller Craig. That provides for issuing bonds outside of the constitutional debt limit in the amount necessary for the construction and equipment of urgently needed new rapid transit lines. These lines would not be self-sustaining at a five-cent fare under the existing legal structure. Therefore, the method is economically impracticable and politically impossible. As noted later, a higher than a five-cent fare is politically impossible. That leaves only the method of reducing costs through modification of the existing legal structure. In this book the writer shows that a five-cent fare is economically possible if the legal structure is modified so that items of expense that are not an actual and necessary part of the cost of carrying a passenger are either reduced or eliminated. To these items, the writer adds taxes. This done, five cents covers the cost of carrying a passenger. That would make $250,000,000 now invested in subways self-sustaining, release that amount of municipal credit from the constitutional debt limit and make it available for new subway construction.

The transit problem can be most clearly stated by putting it in the form in which a syllogism is expressed. It is, therefore, mirrored in the form of a syllogism in what follows:

(1) A five-cent fare is a political necessity.

(2) A self-sustaining fare is a financial necessity because the debt-incurring power of the City that has already been and the additional amount that will be absorbed under Contract No. 3 and Contract No. 4 must be released from the constitutional debt limit before the construction of all of the urgently needed new subways can be financed in harmony with sound business principles.

(3) Therefore, the five-cent fare must be made self-sustaining because that is the only way in which the debt-incurring power (about $300,000,000) noted above can be released from the constitutional debt limit in harmony with sound fiscal principles.

Careful analysis of the political situation shows that the debt-incurring power with which to finance the construction of the urgently needed new subways cannot be made available through a self-sustaining fare if that fare is higher than five cents. But, the same result can be attained if items of expense can be eliminated because they are not germane to carrying passengers and if, in addition thereto, other costs can be reduced in such an amount that a five-cent fare will be *self-sustaining.*

Realization of this situation induced the writer to examine the constitutional, statutory and contractual structure on which rapid transit rests to see if any charges to transit income can be eliminated because it is not necessary to incur them to carry passengers and to study the theory on which rapid transit planning is and has been based to see if it cannot be modified so as to reduce costs. This examination and this study of rapid transit shows that charges to its income can be eliminated and costs can be reduced in the amount necessary to make a five-cent fare self-sustaining, thereby making the revolving fund provision in the constitution again operative, which exempts self-sustaining subway bonds from the constitutional debt limit and, in so doing, make available the municipal credit with which to finance the construction of new subways when and as needed.

This study of the transit situation was ready for publication when the full report of the Board of Transportation as of May 26, 1925, appeared in the press. It impressed upon the writer the necessity of developing more fully than had been done the importance of a correct proportion of trunk and feeder line tracks to each other in the planning of additional transit facilities. To translate this principle into performance to the fullest extent requires a unified system of the new and of the existing rapid transit facilities. Minor changes were incorporated here and there in the analysis so as to make it an up-to-date study as of the date of its release for publication.

During the period in which this book was written, it was the announced intention of the City to recapture Contract No. 3 and Contract No. 4 lines. That policy has been temporarily abandoned for want of cash. It accounts for the attention given to recapture in this study as a method of procedure to establish a municipally owned rapid transit system as distinct from the method of negotiation urged by the writer. That method, in the judgment of the writer, is to be invoked only in the event that negotiation fails and then only to strategic lines as a lesser evil than continuation of the status quo on the existing lines.

In this analysis I. R. T. is an abbreviated expression for Interborough Rapid Transit Company and B. M. T. for the New York Rapid Transit Corporation, operator of the rapid transit lines of the Brooklyn-Manhattan Transit Corporation. Dual Contracts is an abbreviated expression for Contract No. 3 and its related elevated extension certificate, and Contract No. 4 and its related elevated extension and reconstruction certificates.

This study of transit contains more or less repetition. Fundamental principles and important official data are involved in the consideration of a question like this, and, as they have a bearing on the various standpoints from which the question was considered, repetition was inevitable. It would not have been desirable to have avoided it entirely if it could have been done. All minds are not equaly mature and so it may well be that the method of here a little and there a little from different standpoints is the way of correct understanding. As the writer aimed to explain official data repetition became a vital part of his method.

Acknowledgments are due to Michael Goodman and John J. Welsh, accountants, and Benjamin Cohen, former accountant of the Public Service Commission for encouragement and invaluable cooperation. The author is, however, solely and alone responsible for the data embodied and the views expressed in this book.

TABLE *of* CONTENTS

NEW SUBWAYS
A BUSINESS SOLUTION

New Subways
A Business Solution

CHAPTER I.

SUBWAY CONTRACTS BETWEEN CITY AND OPERATING COMPANIES

The City is the owner of the existing subways and has leased them for operation to two companies, namely, the Interborough Rapid Transit Company and the New York Rapid Transit Corporation (a subsidiary of the Brooklyn-Manhattan Transit Corporation). The leases are known as Contract No. 1, Contract No. 2, Contract No. 3 and Contract No. 4.

Under Contract No. 1 and Contract No. 2 the City contributed approximately $65,000,000 for construction of the tubes and viaducts. Under Contract No. 3, the City contributed approximately $92,000,000 and the Interborough Rapid Transit Company approximately $58,000,000 for construction. Under Contract No. 4, the City contributed approximately $135,000,000 toward construction and the New York Rapid Transit Corporation approximately $13,500,000. These data are taken from a report of the Transit Commission dated January

8, 1923. Contract No. 1, Contract No. 2 and Contract No. 3 are with the Interborough Rapid Transit Company and cover equipment by the company and operation to December 31, 1967 except that Contract No. 3 lines are recapturable for municipal operation after ten years of private operation. Contract No. 4 lines are with the New York Rapid Transit Corporation for equipment and operation subject to recapture provisions similar to those of Contract No. 3.

For purposes of operation, Contract No. 3 merges Contract No. 1 and Contract No. 2. The Manhattan Railway through Elevated Extension Certificates, is operated by the Interborough, under lease, in conjunction with the subways leased from the City as a unified system from the standpoint of traffic. Each division (subway and elevated), however, retains the revenue collected on its lines and therefrom deducts the accruals specified in the contracts.

Contract No. 4 and certain Elevated Extension and Reconstruction Certificates are with the New York Rapid Transit Corporation which is the successor of the New York Municipal Railways Corporation and the New York Consolidated Railroad Company. Its stock is owned by the Brooklyn-Manhattan Transit Corporation, successor to the Brooklyn Rapid Transit Company. Contract No. 4 lines are merged with the former elevated lines of Brooklyn for operation through the Elevated Extension and the Reconstruction Certificates noted above.

Contract No. 3 and Contract No. 4, also known as the "Dual Contracts," provide for the equipment and operation of new subways (extensions) by the above noted operating companies in the discretion of the City. If ordered by the local regulatory body they must operate new lines as extensions of existing lines at a single fare from the standpoint of traffic but they may refuse to operate them as component parts of the system until they are self-sustaining, and self-sustaining as defined in the contracts includes interest and sinking fund payments on the City's investment.

CHAPTER II.

NATURE OF THE PREFERENTIAL SYSTEM

The principle underlying the system of revenue distribution embodied in Contract No. 3 and Contract No. 4, is the same except that in Contract No. 3 it is provided that from the pooled revenue derived from operation of Contract No. 1, Contract No. 2 and Contract No. 3 lines the accruals of the City under Contract No. 1 and Contract No. 2 are the first deduction or payment. Then these contracts (Contract No. 3 and Contract No. 4) provide for payment in the following order; rentals that are a company burden, taxes, operating expenses and then of the remainder or operating income the I. R. T. deducts $6,335,000 from its operating income and the B. M. T. deducts $3,500,000 from its operating income.

We will now show how these amounts were computed. They were the operating income of the companies when these contracts were signed, that is, the earnings of these companies on their investment at that time.

The following items from the income statement of the rapid transit division of the B. R. T. as of June 20, 1912 and 1913, will show the source of the $3,500,000 preferential:

1912

Operating revenue		$8,198,741
Operating expenses	$4,113,462	
Taxes	584,456	
Total expenses and taxes		4,697,918
Operating income		$3,500,823

1913

Operating revenue		$8,321,828
Operating expenses	$4,213,563	
Taxes	642,830	
Total expenses and taxes		4,856,393
Operating income		$3,465,435

The $3,500,000 preferential is merely a round number for the operating incomes noted above. It is not a gratuity. It is the operating income as of that time crystallized into a fixed return on the investment of the company as of that time. The book cost of the property of the company as of that time was approximately $57,000,000.

The $6,335,000 of the I. R. T. is similarly derived and is not a gratuity. Its source is given in the table of income statement items which follow:

INCOME STATEMENT ITEMS

Year	Operating Revenue	DEDUCTIONS			Total	Operating Income
		Operating Expenses	Taxes	Contract Nos. 1 & 2 Rentals		
1910	$13,932,506	$4,756,450	$225,280	$2,181,204	$7,162,934	$6,769,572
1911	14,353,206	5,929,653	268,438	2,254,692	8,452,783	5,900,423
Total						$12,669,995
Average per year which is the preferential						$6,335,000

It is thus clear that the $6,335,000 represents the average operating income of the I. R. T. on its subway division for the fiscal years ended June 30, 1910 and 1911, and is merely a return on its then investment and compensation for the risk assumed under Contract No. 1 and Contract No. 2—which were in the nature of a venture.

From what is left after all of the foregoing deductions have been made there are deducted the interest and sinking fund charges of the companies on their additional investments under Contract No. 3 and Contract No. 4. Interest and sinking fund charges on the investment of the City are then deducted. Under Contract No. 3 the City gets 8.76 per cent on its actual investment—the difference between this per cent and actual outlay for interest and sinking fund was incorporated as an offsetting profit to that of the I. R. T. contained in the $6,335,000. Then, after providing a contingency reserve, the unabsorbed balance, if any, was to be shared by the City and the companies on the 50-50 basis. Amounts not earned became unearned preferentials. Those under Contract No. 3 bear interest. Those under Contract No. 4 do not.

In addition the companies can be compelled to operate extensions provided the revenue covers company costs or unearned balances are paid by the City. Owing to the rise in the price of material and cost of labor this provision and the 50-50 profit sharing provision of these contracts are now obsolete due to the fact that if the fare covered the cost of carrying a passenger on extensions the profit on the lines constructed at a lower price level would be prohibitive politically.

As already noted, Contract No. 3 became operative on January 1, 1919, and Contract No. 4 on August 1, 1920. While an appreciable amount of construction had been done before the rise in the price of material and cost of labor due to war and post-war conditions, some of the construction was done and most of the equipment was provided during the period when prices were at their peak. As a result, operating expenses and interest and sinking fund charges are so much higher than estimated when these contracts were signed that unearned preferentials are substantial. That of the subway division of the I. R. T. was $10,434,632.43 as of June 30, 1924; that of the Rapid Transit line of the B. M. T., $15,668,701.45; and that of the City $88,554,620, of which $18,000,000 is included in cost of construction.

Owing to the growth in traffic—excessive density of traffic until new subways are provided—liquidation of the unearned preferentials of the companies is inevitable. The new traffic is carried through the same tubes, over the same viaducts, largely in the same cars and handled largely by the same operating staff. Hence much of the new revenue will be available for liquidation of company unearned preferentials.

Let us examine further the $6,335,000 and the $3,500,000 items. Any extension of a business carries with in an element of venture. This was true of Contract No. 3 and Contract No. 4. As already noted these items were the operating income of the subway division of the I. R. T. and of the rapid transit division of the B. M. T. as of the time these contracts were negotiated.

When one considers that the $3,500,000 was merely the operating income of the rapid transit division of the B. M. T. (then B. R. T.) as of that time crystallized into a fixed income and that that income was merely a return on the then investment and compensation for the risk assumed under Contract No. 4, one must conclude that the charge was not only moderate but was actually inadequate.

Change in the price of material and cost of labor, caused the company to become insolvent. Instead of realizing excessive profits the operating results failed to cover the interest and sinking fund charges on the additional investment of the company since the contract became operative on August 1, 1920. In short, the company deficit was $15,668,701.45 as of June 30, 1924.

As already noted the $6,335,000 deduction from operating revenue is merely the operating income of the I. R. T. as of that time crystallized into a fixed income. From that income, interest and sinking fund charges of the then funded debt has to be deducted to get profit or return on its stock and compensation for managerial ability. Contract No. 1 and Contract No. 2 were ventures. Contract No. 3 too had in it an element of venture. The cumulative deficit thereunder since it became operative on January 1, 1919, was $10,434,623.43

as of June 30, 1924. The company lost approximately $12,000,000 on Contract No. 2 construction; approximately $8,000,000 on the Steinway tunnel extension to Queens, and approximately $20,000,000 on the Queens surface street railway lines which were to be developed as feeders of its projected Queens rapid transit system. In the light of the foregoing, the inclusion of this item in Contract No. 3 was and is a proper charge to revenue and was not unfair to the City or to the travelling public.

The large profits realized under Contract No. 1 and Contract No. 2 between 1913 and the violent rise in price of materials and cost of labor were due to excessive density of traffic because of the failure of the City to construct new subways as needed and so are not a factor that can be considered in the negotiation of Contracts. They were more in the nature of a *treasure trove* than a calculable profit. The amount included in the $6,335,000 in excess of the interest charges as of that time has an offset in the 8.76 per cent allowed the City on its Contract No. 3 investment.

CHAPTER III.

BASIC THEORY UNDERLYING THIS ANALYSIS

In this study, the writer finds no reason to question the tradition associated with transit as a business enterprise that the fare should cover the cost of carrying a passenger. Transit is rather of a class with the telephone, gas and electric light service than in a class with a street and a bridge. It does violence to logic and human experience to view it as akin to a moving bridge. If so, the fare should cover the cost of carrying a passenger and no part thereof should be included in taxes. Because the fare has not covered the cost of carrying a passenger under the Dual Contracts the City lacks the debt-incurring with which to construct urgently needed new subways. The debt-incurring power needed therefor should be made available rather through a fare that will cover the cost of carrying a passenger than through issuance of municipal bonds outside of the constitutional debt limit as proposed by Comptroller Craig and endorsed by the Board of Estimate and Apportionment.

New subway construction of moment, that is, in the amount needed to reduce excessive density of traffic and provide facilities to take care of the growth in traffic requires debt-incurring power additional to that which will accrue from increase in assessment rolls and debt cancellation.

That additional debt-incurring power can only be made available for early use by a program in which it is aimed to make the City's investment under Contract No. 3 and Contract No. 4 self-sustaining. That investment is now approximately $250,000,000.

To make that investment self-sustaining requires either a higher fare on the rapid transit lines so that it will cover the cost of carrying a passenger, or a reduction in the interest charge and modification of the sinking fund provision so that it will be abandoned or charged to taxes.

It is in the interest of the City and of the travelling public that such a fare or such a reduction of the cost of carrying a passenger should be adopted in conjunction with complete municipal ownership of all rapid transit lines and of semi-municipal or 50-50 municipal and private operation through a municipally owned corporation whose directors are appointed by the City and by the investors of transit bonds issued for the property of the operating companies on a 50-50 basis, these directors to elect an additional member who is to serve as chairman.

By amending the State Constitution so that the sinking fund charge for rapid transit bonds will be optional instead of compulsory; also, so that the City can guarantee the principle and interest on transit bonds issued as noted above so that they can be floated at its low rate of interest, the five (5) cent fare can probably be permanently maintained and that without retarding the construction of urgently needed new subways.

In an earlier chapter we described the contracts underlying the income statements of the companies. These income statements mirror the deficit under the existing contractual and legal structure. The income statement for Contract No. 3 includes operation of Contract No. 1 and Contract No. 2; that for Contract No. 4 includes operation of the privately owned Brooklyn elevated lines. In the tabulation which follows we give a consolidated income statement of the result of operation as noted above for the fiscal year ended June 30, 1923—Manhattan elevated not included:

CONSOLIDATED INCOME STATEMENT

Revenue, I. R. T. Subway	$36,344,258.46	
" B. M. T. Rapid Transit	24,722,459.27	
		$61,066,717.73
Operating Expenses, I. R. T. Subway	21,955,138.72	
" " B.M.T. Rapid Transit	15,918,542.55	
Taxes, I. R. T. Subway	450,976.39	
" B. M. T. Rapid Transit	1,351,204.15	
		39,675,861.82
Operating Income		$21,390,855.91
Interest, etc.—I. R. T. Subway	15,518,890.44	
" " B. M. T. Rapid Transit	8,239,589.49	
		23,758,479.93
Unearned preferentials, Company		$2,367,624.02
City interest, etc.—I. R. T. Subway	7,262,040.00	
" " " B. M. T. Rapid Transit	6,916,249.00	
		14,178,289.00
Total unearned preferentials or deficit		$16,545,913.02

The results of operation for the year ended June 30,

1924, do not affect our conclusion and so our earlier tabulations are not changed. In a later chapter we will show that the interest and sinking fund charge on Contract No. 3 and Contract No. 4 lines are materially greater than those of Contract No. 1 and Contract No. 2 per unit of carrying capacity and similarly that the fixed charges on the subway sections of the B. M. T. are materially greater than those of the elevated sections per unit of carrying capacity. This, together with the deficit in the above income statement shows that the recapturable lines of Contract No. 3 and Contract No. 4 cannot be operated at a five-cent fare and cover the cost of carrying a passenger under the existing legal structure.

In order to determine whether a five-cent fare can be maintained under a modified legal structure we must ascertain the nature of the deficit including that of the Manhattan elevated, not included above. This can be done by tabulating the items and, in so doing, show its extent. With these tabulations it can be determined whether any charges can be reduced and whether there are any charges that are not an actual and necessary part of the cost of carrying a passenger.

Analysis of these tabulations will show to what extent charges, if any, can be pruned through supersession of existing securities by municipally guaranteed transit bonds; can be reduced by elimination of taxes through vesting title to all privately owned, non-recapturable lines and rights in the City (City-owned enterprises are not taxed) and by elimination of items that are not a proper charge to transit income. Also, to what extent growth in traffic will contribute thereto and what can be done to make the latter gain permanent through increase of track capacity by lengthening station platforms so that longer trains can be accommodated.

The first section of the tabulation which follows gives the actual deficit as of June 30, 1923. This must be offset if the five-cent fare is to be maintained and the much needed debt-incurring power is to become available with which to construct new subways without delay, other than that which is inherent in the work.

The second section of our tabulation will show that charges can be reduced and others eliminated to such an extent that with the operating economies now in process completed a five-cent fare will cover the cost of carrying a passenger.

(A) Deficits as of June 30, 1923:

(1)	Accruals under Contract No. 3	$8,842,787
(2)	Accruals under Contract No. 4	7,703,127
	Total	$16,500,000
(3)	Includes Municipal profit (about)	3,000,000
	Net deficit	$13,500,000
(4)	Inadequate depreciation	2,300,000
(5)	Manhattan Ry. Dividend—not earned	4,200,000
	Grand Total	$20,000,000

The foregoing tabulation is based on the existing legal structure. It contains items that are not an actual and necessary part of the cost of carrying a passenger.

These items are excluded in the next table. To exclude them requires supersession of the existing legal structure on which transit rests by a legal structure in which title of all privately owned and non-recapturable rapid transit lines and rights will be acquired by the City through a municipally owned corporation in exchange for municipally guaranteed transit bonds issued by this corporation. This plan cannot become operative until January 1, 1928. As of that date, a conservative estimate shows that the existing rapid transit lines can be operated under the new legal structure at a five cent fare with a substantial margin of profit. The second section of our tabulation is as follows:

(B) GAINS THROUGH MUNICIPAL OWNERSHIP AND SEMI-MUNICIPAL OPERATION:

(1)	Sinking fund	$6,000,000
(2)	On interest due to use of municipal credit	4,000,000
(3)	Taxes—City subways are not taxed	4,000,000
(4)	Through better repair and inspection facilities and other economies	3,000,000
(5)	Net income on additional traffic by 1928	5,000,000
	Total	$22,000,000
	Surplus	$2,000,000

It is just possible that $3,000,000 or more may be called from the disbursements through the issue of municipally guaranteed transit bonds to retire the Manhattan, I. R. T., and B. M. T. rapid transit stock, giving an indicated surplus in excess of $5,000,000 as of January 1, 1928, which is the earliest date at which the plan could be made operative. In later chapters, the sections of this plan which are not self-evident will receive elucidation.

The foregoing observations show that charges to income can be reduced to such an extent that a five-cent fare will cover the cost of carrying a passenger on the existing rapid transit lines. But that is not enough. New lines will be constructed and equipped at the prevailing price of materials and cost of labor, that is, at a higher price level.

In a later chapter we will show that one is statistically warranted in inferring that additional lines, when completed, can be operated at a five-cent fare and cover the actual and necessary cost of carrying a passenger if properly articulated with existing lines. In other chapters, we have shown that the taxpayer was placed behind the fare-payer in the Dual Contracts, in order to maintain the five-cent fare. If this policy is adhered to to the extent that deficits in the period in which traffic is developing are charged to taxes, the five-cent fare will cover the actual and necessary cost of carrying a passenger on new and old lines properly coördinated.

In the laying out of new routes dispersion of population has been given great if not controlling weight. This shows that factors other than those of a purely economic character are given consideration in planning an extension or a comprehensive system. Their cost is represented in deficits during the period in which traffic is developing. These are not a proper charge to the cost of carrying a passenger. With this charge and that for a sinking fund eliminated, equipment provided at the low rate of interest of the City and release from taxation (a municipal enterprise is not taxed) a passenger can be carried at a five-cent fare and cover the actual and necessary cost of carrying him on a properly co-ordinated system.

It is impossible to weight the social factors that enter into the selection of a route and attach cost to them. Therefore, initial deficits of an extension are not only a proper charge to taxes but are not a proper charge to the cost of carrying a passenger. The straphanger should not be burdened with this deficit. By including initial deficits in taxes the well-to-do and not the straphanger will pay the bulk of the cost of the dispersion of the City's population by cheap transit to outlying districts.

Clearly deficits on extensions insofar as they are not covered by profits on other parts of the system should be a charge to taxes. That will place the taxpayer behind the farepayer and assure the permanency of the five-cent fare. In this proposal we merely follow the policy underlying the Dual Contracts to its logical conclusion. If the community desires to foster dispersion of population, the cost of such dispersion should be a community burden. Therefore, deficits on extensions should be a fiscal burden until they are extinguished through growth in traffic. Our statistical studies show that before traffic on new lines is developed to capacity, five cents will more than cover the actual and necessary cost of carrying a passenger on a properly planned system.

That dispersion of population is the controlling aim in the laying out of new routes is indicated in the following quotation taken from an address by Chairman McAneny: "The new lines are not laid out to provide paying routes, but to give to the people facilities and to develop all parts of the City in accordance with its natural destiny." Clearly the cost of scattering the population of the City over a wider area should be imposed upon the entire community through charging initial deficits to taxes.

In a later chapter we will show that recapture of Contract No. 3 and Contract No. 4 lines for municipal operation in conjunction with lines to be constructed and equipped is impossible when viewed from the standpoint of traffic. No such objection arises if all rapid transit facilities and rights are acquired by the City through a municipally owned corporation. If the securities issued therefor by this corporation are guaranteed as to principal and interest by the City under proper safeguards, the difference between the annual interest charge for the securities that will be issued and the contractual charge for the company securities now outstanding before the City receives interest and sinking fund payment on its investment under Contract No. 3 and Contract No. 4 will probably be such that that amount at 4½ per cent compound interest will amortize the cost of all the privately owned rapid transit facilities and rights to operate facilities not terminable upon notice in about forty years. The mere fiat of a properly safeguarded municipal guarantee is expected to make such a difference between what will accrue after municipal acquisition and what now accrues that, if set aside as a sinking fund, it will amortize the entire cost. The property acquired will not be paid through change in the fare but through change in the cost of credit. Objections to the acquisition of the elevated lines will be shown, in a later chapter, to be without scientific basis. From this it follows that all privately owned rapid transit facilities and rights should be acquired by the City and be operated by a non-political agency at a five-cent fare.

In the analysis up to this point we have laid the foundation for showing that five cents can be made to cover the actual and necessary cost of carrying a passenger on the rapid transit lines through legal enactments which will permit reduction in the cost of credit (rate of interest) and elimination of other charges not germane to transit as a business enterprise. A sinking fund to amortize liabilities incurred for a revenue producing enterprise like transit is in its nature a philanthropy. Such a philanthropy is a political crime as long as its burden rests exclusively on the straphangers. If the sinking fund policy of today is to be continued then the bulk of its burden should be shifted to the well-to-do and auto-using members of the community through taxes that are in harmony with correct fiscal principles. In a later chapter we will subject the sinking fund provision in the constitution of the State to a searching examination. At this point, we are concerned with the changes in the constitutional and legal structure of the State that are necessary to reduce costs so that five cents will cover the actual and necessary expense of carrying a passenger. In the three paragraphs which follow, we give a condensed statement of these changes:

(1) It is necessary to amend the Transit Commission Law so as to restrict the readjustment plan to the rapid transit lines. In the appraisal of these lines, the officials clothed with authority to deal with the companies for transfer of title of the privately owned and non-recapturable lines to a municipally owned corporation should be vested with discretion so that no legal obstacle will exist to making the plan operative if acquisition on reasonable terms is possible. If such terms can be obtained, it should be possible to exchange existing securities for municipally guaranteed, self-sustaining transit bonds. The Board of Transportation should be vested with authority to arrange the transfer of title, to merge these lines into a going concern and to create the agency to operate the enterprise at cost.

(2) In order to make the foregoing possible, it is necessary to amend the constitution of the State so as to permit the City to guarantee the principal and interest of self-sustaining transit bonds issued by a cor-

poration of which it is the owner in order to make it possible to float them at the low rate of interest that the City enjoys and, in so doing, clothe the revolving fund with a sanction.

(3) In addition to the foregoing, it is further necessary to amend the constitution of the State so that the sinking fund charge on rapid transit bonds issued by the City directly or by a corporation of which it is the owner will be optional instead of compulsory. The sinking fund that exists at the time it takes effect is to be continued as a charge to taxes.

This program calls for two constitutional amendments and one statutory amendment. Their purpose is to effect release from the constitutional debt limit of the $250,000,000 invested by the City under the Dual Contracts so that it can be used for further subway construction. If the Craig plan is adopted to make additional debt-incurring power available for the construction of the urgently needed new subways, the investment will not become self-sustaining unless the fare is raised. Under the law as it now stands, a higher than a five-cent fare will automatically follow when subways constructed and equipped under the Craig plan are in operation three years as they cannot be made self-sustaining under the conditions predicated in the act. But a higher fare in a territory where other lines operate at a five-cent fare is an impossibility. Therefore, deficits would have to be included in taxes. But this could not be done until the act permitting municipal operation is amended. Then the revolving fund would not become operative and so at least another constitutional amendment would become necessary to provide the debt-incurring power with which to construct and equip new subways when and as needed.

The Craig plan is only a palliative—does not effect a settlement of the transit problem. Our plan calls for no greater change in the constitutional and legal structure of the State than the Craig plan and effects a settlement of the transit problem. Under it the officials vested with authority to construct subways are clothed with power to provide the debt-incurring power with which to pay the bills. Its aim is to clothe officials with authority to construct the subways that are needed and not to prevent officials from proceeding with construction to effect transit relief as the existing legal structure of the State does.

The self-sustaining principle which it is sought to embody in the constitutional structure of the State is not to be construed to cover expenditures incurred to foster dispersion of population or any provision for a sinking fund to amortize transit bonds inasmuch as these items are of a fiscal and not of a business character.

CHAPTER IV.

DEBT-INCURRING POWER — ACTUAL AND NECESSARY

The original subway was a venture. It was embarked upon by the City on the theory that its cost could be amortized out of its revenue through a charge thereto for a sinking fund and that when so amortized it would be still as good as new through charges to revenue sufficient to cover obsolescence. Private capital was not available and so credit was secured through use of its debt-incurring power. As new subways can only be provided through further use of the City's debt-incurring power, its status, present and prospective, is now of controlling importance. Comptroller Craig mirrored the situation as of March 1, 1925, in the following:

> According to the revisions made by the Department of Taxes and Assessments in the valuations of real and personal property for taxation in the year 1925, the amount of the increase in the value of real estate effective March 1, 1925, over the valuations for the year 1924 is $752,487,060. There may be some further change in these figures due to mathematical revisions, but any such change will be slight. The effect of this is to increase the City's debt margin by 10 per cent of such sum, or $75,248,706 effective March 1. . . . When tax books were opened [in October] they showed increases in assessed valuations of upward of $1,500,000,000 over

> the valuations for 1924. The estimate made by the Controller at that time was based upon the conclusion that a large part of this increase would be lost in the process of revision, and that the net amount of increase in values available on March 1, 1925, would not increase the city's debt margin by more than approximately $75,000,000.
>
> This conclusion has been fully justified by subsequent events. This increase added to the available debt margin on Jan. 31, 1925, of $33,070,915.64, makes a total on March 1, 1925, of approximately $108,000,000.

Chairman McAneny of the Transit Commission stated in a public address:

> We need $250,000,000 for new subways right away and about $50,000,000 yearly thereafter for further development.

In a statement as of March 15, 1923, he said:

> Nothing could be clearer, therefore, than the fact that there will be no funds available for subways unless the City's needs for schools, docks, and other necessities are set aside or starved down, and that if they were, there would hardly be enough available to make more than a feeble start upon subway building.

In the following statement issued the next day, he mirrored the subway situation with unerring precision:

> The truth of the matter is that the City's present investment of $250,000,000 in [Contract No. 3 and Contract No. 4] subway properties must be placed upon the self-supporting basis through the payment of the incidental annual interest and sinking fund charges from revenue of the road, and similar provision made for the release of future investments, before anything can be done.

In our analysis of the data bearing on debt-incurring power we find that these conclusions of Chairman McAneny are as applicable today as of the date of their publication. The table which follows shows the growth in the number of fare passengers on the combined subway and elevated divisions of the I. R. T.:

PASSENGERS, SUBWAY AND ELEVATED DIVISIONS
1908-1924

Year	*Number of Fare Passengers*	*Increase per cent in 10 years of which this is the last*
1908	483,285,640	....
1909	514,680,342	....
1910	562,788,395	....
1911	578,154,088	....
1912	607,244,697	....
1913	634,316,516	....
1914	651,886,671	....
1915	647,378,266	....
1916	683,752,114	....
1917	763,574,085	....
1918	770,998,335	60 over 1908
1919	809,335,658	....
1920	955,133,110	....
1921	1,013,678,831	....
1922	993,492,690	....
1923	1,025,175,131	....
1924	1,074,343,243	65 over 1914

During the first ten years the number of fare passengers increased approximately 60 per cent and during the last ten years approximately 65 per cent. During the fiscal year ended June 30, 1922, there were approximately 1,000,000,000 fare passengers. If that represented a reasonable density of traffic, then by 1932 or seven (7) years from date of writing there should be completed new subways to handle not less than 600,000,000 additional fare passengers in the I. R. T. territory, that is, the increase after June 30, 1922.

The increase in the number of fare passengers on

the subway division since Contract No. 3 became operative on January 1, 1919 is more marked. The table which follows shows the number of fare passengers by years commencing with the fiscal year ended June 30, 1918:

Fare Passengers, Subway Division, I. R. T.

Year ended June 30:	*Number of Fare Passengers*
1918	418,337,666
1919	461,147,058
1920	586,098,633
1921	639,385,780
1922	644,975,474
1923	676,650,431
1924	714,933,187

The increase in the number of fare passengers during the six (6) years following June 30, 1918 was 296,595,521 or over 70 per cent. During the first four years it was 226,637,808 or over 54 per cent. These percentages show that the 600,000,000 estimated increase in the number of fare passengers during the ten (10) years following June 30, 1922, for new subways additional to the present I. R. T. mileage is statistically warranted if facilities are promptly created in the form of additions to and extensions of the existing systems to handle it. When the saturation point is reached growth in traffic stops and congestion of population instead of dispersion follows.

Testimony at the transit hearing conducted by Judge McAvoy was to the effect that the I. R. T. trunk lines of Manhattan are virtually taxed to their capacity during the morning and evening rush hours. The non-rush period traffic is largely a by-product and bears a rough percentage relation to that of the rush period—reduces the cost of the rush period. Hence, the transit need for Manhattan is for additional trunk lines—one on the east side and one on the west side.

In order to show the meaning of the foregoing figures it is necessary to translate those as of June 30, 1924, into revenue per single mile of track. As of that date, the revenue per single mile of track on the various systems is that given in the statistical summary which follows:

OPERATING REVENUE, YEAR ENDED JUNE 30, 1924

Company	*Operating Revenue*	*Miles of Single Track*	*Revenue per Mile of Single Track*
I. R. T.—Subway	$38,392,635	218	$176,000
I. R. T.—Elevated	19,381,140	123	158,000
B. M. T.—Rapid Transit	27,652,431	263	105,000

In a later chapter we will discuss revenue per mile of single track very fully. Suffice it to say at this point that it depends on the length of station platforms, that is, on length of trains that can be operated during rush hours, on ratio of long-haul and short-haul traffic and on correct proportion of feeder to trunk lines. If station platforms are lengthened on the existing subways as now projected, a density of traffic that will yield $225,000 revenue per mile of single track on both the I. R. T. and B. M. T. subway lines may not be excessive. It may be that on new lines after traffic is developed if the present ratio of feeder to trunk lines is maintained. We will use $225,000 of revenue per single mile of track in our further analysis.

As already noted, there will be an increase of about 600,000,000 fare passengers in the I. R. T. territory by 1932 if provision is made for carrying them. The additional revenue therefrom at a five-cent fare will be about $30,000,000. If $225,000 of revenue per single mile of track represents a reasonable density of traffic after the local stations have been lengthened so that they will accommodate ten-car trains instead of six as at present, then not less than 130 miles of single track should be constructed and be put in operation by 1932 or over 20 miles a year in the territory now served by the I. R. T. Not less than $60,000,000 worth of construction a year is required to take care of this traffic or a total of $360,000,000. This amount may perhaps be reduced more than $60,000,000 if the Washington Heights Line is connected with that of the B. M. T. at 59th Street. To make the debt-incurring power adequate even after release of the investment of the city under Contract No. 3 and Contract No. 4 from the constitutional debt limit requires economy in its use. To link new construction with dead-ended lines gives the maximum of facilities with the minimum of expense.

Contract No. 4 became operative on August 1, 1920. The table which follows shows the number of fare passengers on the B. M. T. Rapid Transit lines by fiscal years commencing with June 30, 1920:

FARE PASSENGERS, B. M. T. RAPID TRANSIT LINES

Year	*Number of Fare Passengers*
1920	376,782,635
1921	414,970,640
1922	444,747,229
1923	480,900,870
1924	537,194,829

The increase is 160,412,194 or on an average of 40,000,000 a year. This is approximately 42 per cent for the period. The subway and original elevated are merged as a traffic agency. Had we subway traffic alone, the per cent of increase would no doubt be as marked as on the subway division of the I. R. T. It would appear that provision should be made to handle an additional 400,000,000 fare passengers by June 30, 1932, for Brooklyn.

We are warranted in concluding from the testimony of Pres. Menden of the B. M. T. that the increase in traffic for Brooklyn can be cared for to June 30, 1932 by the City completing the construction of the lines and facilities outlined under Contract No. 4, by lengthening the stations so that they will accommodate eight car trains instead of six or seven as now and by constructing the Brooklyn Crosstown line as an organic part of the system. If we include therewith a Staten Island passenger subway the cost will be approximately $100,000,000 or about $20,000,000 a year as this construction should be completed in five or six years. This construction completed, provision for post decade growth in traffic will be in order. In short, not less than $20,000,000 a year for construction of new subways for an undetermined period is required for the increase of traffic in Brooklyn. This gives a total of $80,000,000 a year for the metropolitan area as long as traffic increases at the rate it has grown during the last decade.

The increase in the number of fare passengers for the Metropolitan area will be about 1,000,000,000 between 1922 and 1933 if facilities for their conveyance is provided. We noted that the number of fare passengers of the I. R. T. was 1,000,000,000 in 1922 and that that appeared to be a density of traffic that was then in process of becoming excessive. The subway mileage of the I. R. T. is approximately 217. On that amount of mileage and the elevated combined 1,000,000,000 fare passengers were carried during the fiscal year ended June 30, 1922. It appears, therefore, that more than 217 additional miles of new rapid transit lines should be completed by June 30, 1932, unless dead-ended lines are extended into residential districts and station platforms are lengthened. We note elsewhere that the cost of a single mile of subway track will average over $3,000,000. In short, it appears that not less than $400,000,000 should be expended in subway construction by 1930 so that all of it may be equipped and be put in operation not later than 1932.

Owing to its importance we will view the situation from another angle. The number of fare passengers on the subway division of the Interborough Rapid

Transit Company increased at the rate of about 50,-000,000 a year since Contract No. 3 became operative and that of the B. M. T. Rapid Transit Division at the rate of about 40,000,000 a year since Contract No. 4 became operative. The combined increase is now approximately 90,000,000 a year. As all rapid transit trunk lines are now congested, it follows that an amount of mileage that will absorb that amount of additional traffic should be constructed annually. The additional revenue is approximately $4,500,000 a year. If $225,-000 is an indication of a reasonable average density of traffic per single mile of track after stations are lengthened, then 20 miles of new single track should be constructed annually. The cost thereof and of extension of platforms will be not less than $80,000,000 a year for an indeterminate number of years.

This line of reasoning is in harmony with the foregoing that not less than $400,000,000 should be expended in subway construction before January 1, 1930. The traffic situation clearly shows that the City's investment under Contract No. 3 and Contract No. 4 should be made self-sustaining without any unnecessary delay so that that amount of debt-incurring power may become available at the earliest possible moment for new subway construction.

The debt-incurring power available for subway construction depends on policy. If the school building program as announced from time to time is carried out, not enough will be available at least during 1926 and 1927.

According to the Public Education Association, "The number of children on part time or double sessions" in the City schools was 118,207 in September, 1917; 377,794 in September, 1923, and 317,891 in September, 1924. Mayor Hylan's platform called for "A seat for every child." The Board of Education has an organization for "plan production" that can turn out plans for new school buildings at a rate that will absorb more than 50 per cent of the debt-incurring power that will accrue. Therefore, the amount of debt-incurring power that will be technically available during 1925-1927 is no evidence that that amount can, will or should be devoted to subway construction. The use to which the available debt-incurring power will be put will depend on public pressure. The members of the Board of Estimate are virtually pledged to make the appropriations that the Board of Education can use. It is, therefore, probable that appropriations for new school buildings will be as large as political exigencies will permit.

The amount of debt-incurring power available for actual subway construction is materially affected by the fact that the full amount involved is deducted at the signing of a contract although it may take two, three or four years to complete the work. Comptroller Craig brought this out in his testimony at the transit hearing conducted by Judge McAvoy with marked precision. It is contained in the following:

> **Delaney's plan calls for the expenditure of $60,000,000 for subway construction in 1925. Or, rather, contracts for this amount will be let this year under his plan.**

It makes no difference whether all that money is paid out in 1925 or not; once a contract is validated the total amount must be provided for it under the city's debt limit, even though payments on that contract may run for several years. Consequently, although the Board of Transportation may only spend $20,000,000 in 1925, the Department of Finance must deduct the face value of the contracts from the full limit of the city's available credit."

We stress this fact because of the prevailing misconception. It makes an ambitious report of a semi-civic organization worse than worthless. In the following, we reproduce a section of this report:

The margin of borrowing power available within the next few years is ample, if it be conserved and used only for new transit construction and other necessary projects. On Jan. 1, the unreserved margin was almost $50,000,000. It is estimated that on March 1 about $75,000,000 additional will be available from the increase in real-estate assessments. This gives a total of over $125,000,000 for this year.

Controller Craig has estimated that an average of approximately $35,000,000 annually will be available from budget appropriations for redemption and amortization of the debt, plus sinking fund earnings. To this should be added the power to incur debt, estimated at $50,000,000 or $55,000,000 yearly, coming from subsequent annual increases in the assessed value of reality. It thus appears that with the sum of $125,000,000 available this year and annual additions from $85,000,000 to $90,000,000 to the borrowing power, there should be ample funds for all municipal capital outlays, including subway building, without increasing the debt limit.

It will be impossible to complete the construction of the requisite new subway systems in less than 6 years. There is enough money now available, or will be after March 1, 1925, to meet this year's requirements in full. The cost of construction payable each year thereafter can be adequately met from each year's normal increase of the borrowing power, due to the increased assessment valuation of real estate arising in the main from improvements in outlying territory.

Compare this quotation with the above quotation from

the testimony of Comptroller Craig. Its significance can be made manifest through quotations from the testimony of Mr. Ridgway, Chief Engineer of the Board of Transportation, at the transit hearing conducted by Judge McAvoy. The first part of the testimony relates to the Fourteenth Street-Eastern Line and is as follows:

SHERMAN: How long a time in your judgment is it going to take to finish this line?

RIDGWAY: Probably three years for the construction, and another year for track, station finish and equipment.

SHERMAN: So it will take substantially four years from the time the last contract is let; is that what you mean to say?

RIDGWAY: The last contract will be let, I assume during a somewhat shorter time than those that are now let.

The following testimony relates to the Washington Heights line:

SHERMAN: You have stated that it would take four years, I believe, to build the Washington Heights Line?

RIDGWAY: Yes, sir, three years for the construction and about a year for station finish and equipment.

SHERMAN: That would have to be dated from the time the contracts were awarded?

RIDGWAY: Yes, sir.

SHERMAN: And how long a time will elapse before the plan of the road is complete so that those contracts can be advertised?

RIDGWAY: We expect to have them in six months. I might say this, to qualify that, that some of the sections will take longer to construct than others, and we are endeavoring to get those that will take longer under contract first.

While these lines were penned (March 14, 1925) ground was broken for the construction of two sections of the Washington Heights Line. This enables us to illustrate the fact we are stressing. From an evening paper of that day the excerpt which follows was taken:

> The Mayor broke ground for the section which is under contract to Heyman & Goodman. This section is known as Section 3 of Route 78, and extends from 111th Street and Eighth Avenue to 122nd St. and St. Nicholas Avenue. The section being dug by the Rosoff concern is Section 3A of Route 78 and extends from 122nd Street and St. Nicholas Avenue to 133rd Street. The contracts for both sections aggregate $9,598,036.

This line will not be ready for operation until 1930 at the earliest. The full amount noted above has been deducted from the debt-incurring power of the City. At least two-thirds of this amount will be moribund for twelve months and of that amount one-third or more for another twelve months if construction is completed in 1928.

During the first year of a contract from 50 per cent to 75 per cent of the debt-incurring power involved will be moribund. If $75,000,000 of debt-incurring power is absorbed only $25,000,000 may be consumed during the first year and $50,000,000 be moribund. Because of this fact, nearly $150,000,000 debt-incurring should be available in 1926 and in 1927, and about $50,000,000 additional to that which accrues for two or three years thereafter. If transit relief is to be expedited approximately $150,000,000 debt-incurring power should be made available in excess of that which accrues under the existing constitutional and legal structure in 1926 and 1927.

Now turn to the last sentence of the quotation from the semi-civic organization and in the light of the Craig and Ridgway testimony you will no doubt agree with the writer that the cost of construction payable each year thereafter cannot be adequately met from each year's normal increase of the borrowing power because some of it will have to be paid out of debt-incurring power that had accrued when the contract was signed—one, two or three years earlier.

It is not practicable to make sections so small that their construction can be completed in one year. Therefore, in order to get the amount of construction that should be done in 1926 and 1927, actually done, it is necessary to place twice or thrice that amount under contract in those years and for that the debt-incurring power accruing is inadequate.

We are clearly warranted in concluding that the subways which should be ready for operation by or before 1932 should be placed under contract not later than 1928, that is, contracts in the amount of $400,000,000. Construction costing that amount should be practically completed by the end of 1930 as it will take a year or more for installation of equipment.

During the period in which this amount should be available for contracts for subway construction not less than $150,000,000 will be required to complete the school building program. Approximately $550,000,000 will be needed by 1928 if proper progress is to be made in the construction of new subways and in the erection of new school buildings—other needs being financed on the pay-as-you-go plan.

The foregoing observations about subway construction

and the erection of new school buildings mirrors the amount of debt-incurring power that will be needed if headway is to be made in removing objectionable conditions. We will now show the amount that will become available through normal accruals.

As of March 1, 1925, there was $108,000,000 of unused debt-incurring power. During the three years 1926-1928, about $112,000,000 will become available from debt cancellation and the writer estimates that probably less than $150,000,000 will accrue from increase in assessment rolls. This gives us a total of $370,000,000 or about $180,000,000 less than the amount needed. Accruals from debt cancellation in 1929 and 1930 and from increase in assessment rolls during the same period will not be available for construction of subways that are to be ready for operation in 1930-1931.

During 1926 and 1927, the amount of debt-incurring power that will become available will probably be less than $85,000,000 a year, while the amount needed for actual construction and reservations for contracts that are to be completed two or more years later should be about $150,000,000 a year. If this amount is not available, subway construction and erection of school buildings in the amount urgently needed will be delayed.

Our analysis shows that during a period in which not less than $550,000,000 is needed probably less than $370,000,000 will become available through normal accruals. Clearly debt-incurring power other than that which accrues under the existing legal structure is needed if subway construction and the erection of school buildings are to be prosecuted without delay, other than that which is inherent in the nature of the work.

We have already noted the need for additional school buildings. It is as great if not greater than that for new subways. Note the following from the inaugural address of Superintendent O'Shea:

> We have been making strides in recent years in providing better housing for the children in school. We shall need to keep on building more schools and completing them more rapidly. It is important not alone that we shall house our children decently but we should also strive to reduce steadily the number of over-large classes, seeking to achieve a condition where no class in the public schools shall have more than forty-five children.

Also the following from an editorial on the address of George J. Ryan on being re-elected president of the Board of Education last May (1924):

> Mr. George J. Ryan, in his address on being re-elected President of the Board of Education, dwelt chiefly upon the building program. A year ago [1923] it was estimated that nearly $200,000,000 would be required to eliminate part-time and double or duplicate sessions and to provide seats necessary to meet the increases in the September register for the next five years. According to President Ryan's statement, the present building program provides for 210 new school buildings at a cost of $150,277,514. This amount added to what has been spent since May of 1923 will make a total approximating the enormous sum estimated to be needful to catch up with the increased school population. But even so, no allowance is made for reducing oversized classes, nor for the replacement of temporary wooden buildings or of buildings constructed fifty years or more ago. Unless, therefore, funds beyond the total named are available under the present educational policy, objectionable conditions will still exist.

A news item as of April 17, 1925, indicates that the

amount that is being spent in the construction of new school buildings is probably in excess of $40,000,000 a year. It is mirrored in a $60,000,000 offering of serial bonds by Controller Craig. The excerpt which follows is taken from the announcement:

> The bonds will bear interest at the rate of 4¼ per cent., payable semi-annually. The entire issue is made for the purpose of construction of new schools and the acquisition of sites.
>
> This issue will not increase the city's debt in any particular. The proceeds will be used to take up outstanding short-term notes issued by the Controller at the low rates prevailing during the past year.

The building program of the Board of Education is endorsed by the Commissioner of Education of the State of New York. If carried out as projected, there will not be nearly enough debt-incurring power available for subway construction for a number of years. It should be carried out or children will be deprived of that which is the birthright of every child—that education which best prepares it for life. It is *now* that additional school buildings are needed. These can be provided only through use of the current and prospective increase in debt-incurring power. They can be provided in no other way. Not so with new subways. They can be provided by making the investment of the City under Contract No. 3 and Contract No. 4 self-sustaining.

It is a sad commentary on the schools of the largest city in the world that the best that can be aimed at are classes not in excess of forty-five. That is an excessive number. Hence, should a more extensive use be made of the work-study-play rotation in the future, reduction in the size of classes will absorb rooms that might be in excess were the rotation adopted with classes up to forty-five.

If the foregoing analysis is correct, not less than $80,000,000 a year should be used in actual subway construction annually and not less than $40,000,000 a year in the erection of school buildings. In an ambitious article published in the Times on March 1, 1925, we are told "Contractors would find it difficult to do $45,000,000 of work a year." It is further contended that that amount is available from the annual accruals in debt-incurring power and that resort to constitutional amendment is unnecessary.

Experience shows that the building trade can absorb more than $40,000,000 a year in the construction of school buildings. We are, however, prompted by the foregoing challenge to make a further examination of the amount of debt-incurring power needed for subway construction. The table on the number of fare passengers which follows is taken from the McAvoy transit report—totals are supplied by the writer:

GROWTH IN THE NUMBER OF FARE PASSENGERS

Fiscal Year Ended June 30	*Interborough Subway Lines*	*B.M.T. Rapid Transit Lines*	*Total*
1918	418,000,000	258,000,000	676,000,000
1919	461,000,000	309,000,000	
1920	586,000,000	377,000,000	
1921	640,000,000	405,000,000	
1922	645,000,000	445,000,000	
1923	677,000,000	481,000,000	
1924	715,000,000	537,000,000	1,252,000,000
Increase			576,000,000

This gives an average increase of 96,000,000 fare passengers a year or an increase of 85 per cent for the 6 years. On that increase of traffic, $4,800,000 additional passenger revenue was collected per year. Assume that $225,000 per single mile of track can be collected on the new lines due to longer station platforms, larger cars and longer trains. Even under those circumstances approximately 20 miles of new track should be constructed annually to accommodate the increase in the number of fare passengers. Thereto, an additional amount must be added to reduce the existing congestion. If construction is largely of the trunk line or under river tunnelling character it will cost over $3,000,000 per single mile of track—the total for the new traffic and the extra construction to relieve congestion will mount to $80,000,000 a year for a period of years. To get under contract enough so that that amount of construction will be done annually requires about $150,000,000 debt-incurring power a year in 1926 and 1927.

If it is impossible to do that amount of digging annually then the City is unable to provide for its growth. It is the function of analysis to point out the extent of the need and the cost to provide the facilities. If Contractors cannot expand their organizations sufficiently to do the work then the City is doomed to intolerable traffic conditions. It is, however, a probability amounting to a certainty that the facilities with which to construct the additional transit facilities that are needed for the growth of the City will be created as soon as an effective demand therefor exists.

Chairman McAneny sensed the situation correctly when he said that the City needed $250,000,000 at once for subway construction and $50,000,000 annually thereafter. In this study, we are pointing out how the $250,000,000 can be made available during the next three years in addition to the accruals heretofore noted.

Let us picture to ourselves a competent committee passing judgment on the questions involved. Such a committee would consist of an eminent financier, an engineer who is a traffic expert, an expert in educational psychology and a specialist in sociology. The financier would hold that the investment of the City under Contract No. 3 and Contract No. 4 should be made self-sustaining through the adoption of a flexible fare so that it would be automatically changed when necessary to cover the cost of carrying a passenger. The traffic expert would hold that the debt-incurring power thereby liberated should be used as quickly as possible in the construction of new subways. The expert in educational psychology would hold that as much as needed of the current unused debt-incurring power with increases due to increase in the assessment roll should be used in the construction of additional school buildings until the urgently needed school facilities are available. The sociologist would hold that the fare should be the same on all transit facilities engaged in mass transportation so that dispersion of the population may be induced and concentration or congestion discouraged. From this and earlier observations it appears that the bulk of the debt-incurring power with which to construct new subways should be derived by making the investment of the City under Contract No. 3 and Contract No. 4 self-sustaining.

It is a condition and not a theory which confronts the City. It is not what ought to have been done but what was done that gives the facts that control judgment. It is not what should be done but what will be done that has a bearing on new subway construction. The new school buildings that will be erected should be erected. If the investment of the City under Contract No. 3 and Contract No. 4 is made self-sustaining that debt-incurring power can be used only for new subway construction. It should be made available without any unnecessary delay.

In this chapter, our calculations presume continuance of the existing ratio between trunk lines and feeder lines and of long haul to short haul traffic. To the extent that that ratio may be modified in future planning so that all parts of the system may be operated nearer to capacity than at present to that extent our base figure, $225,000 in revenue per single mile of track, will have to be modified. This aspect of the transit situation is treated at length in Chapter XV.

CHAPTER V.

DEBT-INCURRING POWER AND MUNICIPAL FINANCE

Not only are new lines to be constructed but Contract No. 3 and Contract No. 4 lines are to be recaptured. If the status of debt-incurring power is as shown in this analysis of the transit situation then acquisition and operation of the recapturable rapid transit lines by the City adds to the transit fantasy. This calls for further analysis of debt-incurring power. Debt-incurring power is contingent upon assessed valuation. In theory and under the law assessment of real estate is at its market value so that the burden of taxation may be equitably distributed. In practice, there is inequality and undervaluation. But the State Board of Equalization passes on the assessment roll of local departments and so the inference is warranted that assessed values approximately represent market value. Hence, additional debt-incurring power of moment cannot be secured by a horizontal levelling up of real estate values in assessment and so can only be secured through new construction and development of unimproved areas. That will not provide much more than the debt-incurring power needed for municipal needs other than subways and so the transit situation cannot be materially affected thereby. Even this is not all. When Europe has been rehabilitated sufficiently to transact business on a gold basis, gold will have been absorbed for their bank reserves in a volume possibly as great if not greater than before the world war. During the reconstruction period, our excess gold supply will be shunted to Europe. That will make gold relatively scarcer. Gold coin will as a consequence rise in value. The consequence of this is fall in prices and wages. The effect of this is fall in the value of buildings constructed at a higher price level. Fall in the value of buildings means decrease in assessed value as property cannot be legally assessed higher than the current market value.

Ambassador Kellogg on his return from abroad stated:

> The Dawes plan has had much to do with the stabilization of the currency of Europe. Germany is now on a gold basis. England will soon be. South Africa goes on a gold basis July 1, and many of the smaller countries of Europe are approaching the gold standard. There is nothing of greater importance to the American people than that Europe and in fact all the world should go back to the gold basis. Fluctuating currencies make it impossible to carry on commerce, and as the United States has always been on a gold basis it is good to have the whole world on that basis.
>
> Another thing: People of Europe whom I have met myself realize that there is no short cut or magic cure for the evils growing out of the great war and that restoration can come only by thrift and economy in private enterprise and in Government budgets.

Passions aroused by the world war are subsiding. Readjustment is speeding up. As a result the volume of business will grow. Gold is already flowing abroad. As soon as it will reduce our active reserves the value of gold will increase which is in effect a fall in the price level.

Deferred erection of buildings on account of the world war has been almost entirely made up. After it is entirely made up, the increase in assessment rolls will only be that due to construction called for by the normal growth in population, less recession in the value of buildings erected at the present price level and obsolescence of other buildings. In short, the heretofore appreciation in value due to change in the value of gold coin will be followed by depreciation in value due to the reverse change in the value of gold coin. We know the extent of the depreciation of gold. We cannot forecast the extent of its appreciation. That there will be some rise in the value of gold coin and per contra fall in the price level is a probability amounting to a certainty.

Viewing the situation from the standpoint of current practice of loaning institutions gives the same result. They loan only forty (40) per cent of the appraised value of new buildings on first mortgage. Why? Because they expect recession in prices and in the compensation paid to labor. That means fall in the value of buildings constructed at the present price level and a corresponding reduction in assessed values. Will new construction and development of unimproved areas offset the fall in the value of buildings constructed at a higher price level? Time will tell. That it will put an added strain on the finances of the City already under stress is a conclusion fortified by economic experience. These observations show that caution is necessary in the further use of the debt-incurring power of the City.

In our analysis so far we have assumed that probably less than $50,000,000 debt-incurring power will accrue annually from increase in the assessed value of the real estate in the City. It appears that deferred construction due to world war and post war conditions is about made up except for tenements at a moderate rental. Even with excess construction due to the above conditions, there accrued only $55,000,000 debt-incurring power in 1924 and $75,000,000 in 1925.

The estimated cost of buildings for which permits were issued is a barometer. Those for the quarter ended March, 1925, fell short of those for the quarter ended March, 1924, by about $160,000,000 in this city. That there is a slowing up in building construction is asserted by former Senator Calder, a builder, in the following:

> Only a normal business should be expected this year, however. Don't let any one tell you there is going to be another boom in building. We have caught up. There is only one class of building in which we are behind—homes for the worker who has a wage of $40 a week or less. That sort of construction is impossible in Manhattan. It costs too much.

Mr. McIlvain of Babson's Statistical Service says: "I believe that the peak of the building activity has been passed and that the business will adjust itself to normal conditions." This is in line with the best thought of today in this city. If there is a slowing up in building activity and if, as a result, less than $50,000,000 debt-incurring power accrues from increase in real estate assessments after this year, that amount ought to be absorbed in the construction of new school buildings. That leaves only accruals through debt cancellation. As much debt-incurring power as possible should be conserved.

The conclusion is warranted that no more debt-incurring power than is absolutely necessary, should be earmarked: Usable only for subway construction. If the investment of the City under Contract No. 3 and Contract No. 4 is made self-sustaining some of the accruing debt-incurring power can be conserved for other major municipal needs such as opening of new avenues for vehicular traffic which cannot be deferred much longer.

CHAPTER VI.

MUNICIPAL OPERATION VERSUS SEMI-MUNICIPAL OPERATION

Semi-municipal operation merges the operating efficiency of private enterprise with the low rate of interest of the City. Under it the operating personnel of the existing companies would be continued. Are these operating staffs efficient? On this point, disinterested expert opinion is the sole guide. That of Isidor Fraser of the Underground Electrical Railways of London meets the test. In an interview published in the press of this City he said:

> The whole trouble here, in my opinion, is that the five (5) cent fare is eternally made a political issue. Now it has been our experience that there is an economic fare which is set in reality by the public, with which it is dangerous to tamper. The economic level finds itself. It is just as ridiculous to set an abitrary flat rate of five (5) cents for distances varying from a quarter of a mile to twenty-eight miles as it would be to sell all cigars at a flat five (5) cent fare. It is, in my opinion, impossible for traction companies to operate successfully on this basis.
>
> Transport must show a reasonable good return in order to attract private capital. Unless you in New York are able to work out some kind of system whereby traction concerns can operate on a paying basis you are drifting toward chaos. It may be a little difficult to work the zone system for regulating fares as we do in London, but a varying rate commensurate with the distance travelled ought in some way to be managed.

> Your subway is, it seems to me, run very efficiently, considering the difficulties it has to contend with. But you need more express subways, and you can get these only when a reasonable return on the investment is assured. But heaven help you if you get municipal ownership [operation].

Equally convincing is the following clipping from a local paper:

> Before sailing yesterday for Southampton on the White Star liner Olympic, Lord Ashfield, Chairman of the Underground Electric Railways of London, said that New York had the finest transit system in the world. Lord Ashfield said he made frequent trips in the subways while here and found them "amazingly efficient." New York might well be proud of its rapid transit system, he added, and, although it is true that the subways are overcrowded, "nevertheless I've never seen trains dispatched with such speed."

Semi-municipal operation is a new type of enterprise that is worth while trying out in the public utility field. Regulation of public utilities does not keep down cost of service as far as possible if the rate of return is fixed by a Commission. Operating expenses have a tendency to be shifted upward through excessive liberality to officers and employees.

If this type of enterprise should prove as successful in practice as it is attractive in theory it may well be that extension of it to public utility enterprises would follow. It provides for supersession of regulation, operation at cost by a board of control on which the public on the one hand and the security holders on the other are represented on a 50-50 basis with a Chairman elected by them. If this should actually merge in practice as it does in theory the efficiency of private enterprise with the low charge for credit of the municipality its extension to other public utilities would be assured.

Municipal operation is associated in the public mind with inefficiency. Over twenty-three years' experience as a civil service employee has satisfied the writer that there would be more sinecures and greater inefficiency under municipal than under private operation and that the tendency would be for operating expenses to grow faster than the growth in revenue would warrant.

The conclusion stated in the foregoing paragraph is forcefully expressed in an article by Pres. Butler of Columbia University which appeared in "The Woman Republican." The part which is apropos here is as follows:

> The elements of this question are few and simple. Probably the credit of the City is necessary to the development of an adequate system of rapid transit within the city limits. But municipal operation of that system would mean waste, extravagance and the building up of a huge political machine that might well be the City's ruin.

In the situation under discussion, the question is not merely which mode of operation is preferable. Semi-municipal operation stands, in this instance, for a unified operation and a single system while municipal operation is predicated on four separate systems operated independently of each other. We will note here in addition economies in the use of facilities if a unified rapid transit system is adopted and semi-municipally operated. The following from the minutes of the transit hearing conducted by Judge McAvoy is to the point:

Sherman — What about the capacity of the Broadway Line—I call it the Broadway Line; I mean the Broadway-Seventh Avenue to 59th Street—to accommodate the increased volume of traffic that would be poured into it from Washington Heights?

Menden—Additional traffic coming to the Broadway Line from an extension north of 59th Street would fit in very nicely with the traffic now carried on the Broadway Line; because the traffic Northbound in the evenings on two tracks—or at least on one track—is very light, and we could conveniently carry all the traffic that would come to that line from two tracks of the extension north of 59th Street, without adding any additional cars to that service. The additional cars would be only required to run a line north, depending on how far it ran north.

In the morning, our trains south bound on one of our tracks, at least, is negligible because the traffic that we carry, we carry northward. Therefore, any passenger traffic that would originate north of 59th Street could be very conveniently carried on those trains. Therefore, it is reasonable to assume that all of the traffic of the extension to Washington Heights that could be carried on two tracks could be very conveniently carried on the Broadway subway, without adding any cars or trains to that service south of 59th Street.

Prof. Pupin of Columbia University, inventor and scientist, stated the case against municipal operation of public utilities with precision and directness at a luncheon of the Rotary Club. An excerpt from a press report of this address will serve as an admirable conclusion to this chapter. It is reproduced in the following quotation:

Nobody will deny the knowledge which enables us in trade competitions to do things just a little better than anybody else, and in times of war to establish our superiority over the enemy by superior skill, intelligence and scientific organization, but there is another aspect in the recent activities of our scientific and industrial organizations, and it is this: The great achievements in cooperation between science and industries is a living illustration of what can be accomplished when the great problems of science and of the industries are entrusted to the intelligent care of trained hands and superior intelligence. This illustration will soon demonstrate, even to a mediocre mind, that it is not true that any man can do any job, as those who control political patronage seem to think. There are many, many things which Tom, Dick and Harry cannot do; they lack both intelligence and training.

The weakest point in democracy has always been lack of appreciation of expert knowledge. Railroads, telegraphy, telephony and radio broadcasting, electrical lighting and electrical transmission of power are certainly public utilities, but the intelligent people of the United States will never consent that these things, requiring an enormous amount of expert knowledge, be placed under Government ownership. The machinery of our Government or of any other form of government known to man today is utterly incapable of handling technical problems which require the highest type of training applied to the highest type of intelligence.

All of these public utilities are full of complex technical problems which cannot and never were intended to be handled by any Government. In Europe we see that where there is governmental ownership the utilities are being run at heavy deficits. And only recently Mussolini has said that he wants to get away from Government ownership and adopt the American system.

We have now made the necessary basic studies so that the reader will more easily see the reason for the readjustments suggested. We will first discuss the legal enactments that are necessary to effect a reduction in the charge for the use of money and the agency through which to give it expression.

CHAPTER VII.

MUNICIPAL GUARANTEE OF TRANSIT BONDS

Under the Transit Commission plan, title to all serviceable transit lines is to be vested in a municipally-owned corporation, modelled after the Emergency Fleet Corporation of the Federal Governmnt, which is to issue therefor self-sustaining transit bonds. These bonds are to bear interest at five per cent and are to be amortized through a sinking fund in thirty-eight (38) years. The plan proposed herein applies the operating principles noted above to the rapid transit lines only. As these lines will then be the property of the City, and will be operated at a self-sustaining fare, there can be no valid objection to the City guaranteeing both their principal and interest, and, in so doing, make it possible to float them at its low rate of interest. This will save the City the difference between the interest rate essayed to be paid by the Transit Commission or that paid at present by the companies and that of the City.

It would appear that such a guarantee is a carollary of the municipal ownership and semi-municipal operation plan proposed by the Transit Commission. If so, it is a carollary of the plan proposed herein, which is that of the Transit Commission restricted to the rapid transit lines merged with the low rate of interest feature in the program of Mayor Hylan.

In short, it is merely proposed that the City guarantee its *de facto* liabilities that are a legal claim against the property purchased therewith so that it will get the credit with which to purchase, through the above noted corporation, the privately owned rapid transit lines or facilities at the low rate of interest of its bonds that are a deduction from the debt limit. They will be simply another variety of municipally self-sustaining obligation issued outside of the debt limit accompanied by a proviso that the property acquired therewith must be operated at a fare that will keep it self-sustaining.

Issuance of self-sustaining transit bonds through a municipally owned corporation rather than direct issue outside of the constitutional debt limit creates an agency for coupling the operating efficiency of private enterprise with the low interest rate of the City. It sidesteps municipal operation and furnishes a basis for 50 per cent representation on the Board of Control by directors elected by the security holders. It adds municipal guarantee of principal and interest to self-sustaining transit bonds, such as the Transit Commission essayed to issue, to reduce the interest charge and to clothe the revolving fund with a sanction that will permanently put the burden of transit on passengers and prevent inclusion of deficits in taxes.

It was the intent and purpose of the revolving fund provision when it was incorporated in the debt limit article of the Constitution to enable the City to create and maintain an adequate transit system with only a nominal amount of debt-incurring power earmarked: Usable only for subway construction. The provision is not mandatory. The guarantee for transit bonds proposed herein will supply the sanction. Action on the part of the responsible officials will thereafter be mandatory. They will be compelled thereafter to adjust the fare so that it will cover the cost of carrying a passenger. This fare will be given quasi-stability through a flexible sinking fund. This provision in its application, will have an identical effect on all subway bonds and so make and keep them all self-sustaining as they are all issued for the property of a single traction system. In short, it supplies the link which will make and keep the revolving fund provision of the Constitution operative.

The Transit Commission in its plan contemplated floating a type of security unknown to the investing public. Attach to that security the guarantee of principal and interest by the City and you add to it greater marketability. This guarantee by the City of a *de facto* liability of its own not deductible from the debt limit is the one additional step necessary to make possible the maintenance of the five-cent fare on a self-sustaining basis—supersession of which is not politically possible at this time.

The transit deadlock can be ended only if costs are reduced so that the nickle will do. The converging effect in 1928, of virtual abandonment of the sinking fund, as a charge to transit income, lower interest rate due to municipal guarantee of the principal and interest of the transit bonds heretofore noted, substantial economies due to further installation of labor-saving devices, exemption from taxes as is the City's investment in the present subways, and the large profit on the traffic additional to that of the present volume, will simultaneously reduce costs and increase revenue to such an extent that the net result will be that a five-cent fare will cover the cost of carrying a passenger on the existing lines and permit the accumulation of substantial depreciation and contingency reserves.

But the amendment permitting the City to guarantee both principal and interest of bonds issued to acquire the privately owned rapid transit facilities and rights can be drawn so that if the five-cent fare again becomes inadequate, its supersession by a fare that will be adequate, will be automatic. Guaranteeing self-sustaining transit bonds does not differ vitally from exempting self-sustaining subway bonds from the debt limit. It merely adapts the procedure to conditions created by the world war.

Modification of the sinking fund requirement and sanctioning of the City guaranteeing self-sustaining transit bonds issued by a municipally owned corporation is not as great an innovation as municipal operation of new subways at a five-cent fare for an initial period of three years and then amortizing the accumulated deficit through charges to revenue during the next ten years. These revolutionary provisions are contained in the law which created the Board of Transportation.

Why should the City pay a higher interest rate for the 50 per cent liability of a property that it owns through a municipally owned corporation than for the other 50 per cent that it owns directly and will lease to this corporation? Both are issued for a property that can be and should be kept self-sustaining. To ask the above question in the way in which it is asked is to answer it. The logic of the situation requires that these mounting millions be saved through the municipal guarantee herein outlined.

This program calls for purchase, through negotiation, of the privately owned rapid transit facilities and of the rights to operate facilities that are not recapturable, that is, leases that are not terminable upon notice. We observed in the preface that the fair value of these facilities and rights is the actuarial value of the earnings under the preferential system at a five-cent fare for the securities that are a lien thereon or represent ownership thereof. The income provided therein is earned at present save that that paid on Manhattan Railway stock is not earned by the elevated division. The fact that the contractual income is earned as noted above coupled with the strategic position of the companies in the transit situation makes the actuarial value, actual and potential, of the earnings the actual value of the facilities and rights. When all the factors in the situation are marshalled that are necessary for judgment one is forced to conclude that the maximum compensation that the City can be forced to pay and the minimum that the companies can be forced to accept are virtually the same, that is, the actuarial value of the earnings which attaches to the securities for which municipally guaranteed transit bonds are to be issued in exchange in the transfer of title to the above noted transit facilities and rights. That is due to the preferential system of revenue distribution contained in the contracts between the City and the companies. The contractual provisions for the distribution of the earnings of the companies are the key to the solution of the transit problem. Until that fact is recognized no headway can be made in removing intolerable traffic conditions. These observations show that supersession of company securities by municipally guaranteed transit bonds on the terms indicated herein is mutually advantageous and therefore seemingly capable of being translated into performance.

In order to make virtually impossible subway planning that is not in harmony with the underlying principles of this program the constitution of the State should be amended so that the two per centum of the assessment roll to which taxes are limited will include deficits on municipally owned revenue producing enterprises. That aspect of the transit problem can be most advantageously considered at this point.

It appears to be the opinion of a civic organization which has made an extended study of the transit situation that the *two per centum* to which the tax rate is restricted by the Constitution of the State may force adoption of a self-supporting fare when new subways are ready for operation. It may be inferred from the following excerpt from a leaflet that it issued recently:

> The proposed new subways will have a less dense traffic and consequently reduced earnings. It is probable, therefore, that the greater part of the annual fixed charges of $39,000,000 will constitute a deficit to be paid by taxation. The amount which the City may raise by taxation for its current expenses in any one year is restricted by the Constitution to 2 per cent of the assessed valuation of its real and personal estate. This limit has already practically been reached, even on the present basis of City expenses. No suggestion has yet been made as to how the City can obtain by taxation perhaps $35,000,000 additional to pay a subway deficit, and still keep within the constitutional tax limit.

We will give the provision in the constitution to which this paragraph refers so that the reader will be able to verify the matter. That provision reads as follows:

> The amount hereafter to be raised by tax for county or city purposes, in any county containing a city of over one hundred thousand inhabitants, or any such city of this state, in addition to providing for the principal and interest of the existing debt, shall not in the aggregate exceed in any one year two per cent of the assessed valuation of the real and personal estate of such county or city, to be ascertained as prescribed in this section in respect to county or city debt.

In a morning paper or an evening paper during the week commencing February 16, you will find that the tax rate for the ensuing year is 2.68. Comptroller Craig states it as follows: "The general tax rate in all boroughs for 1925 will be 2.68. This is a reduction of 5 points from the base rate of 2.73 levied for 1924." If thereto a small per cent is added for local taxes we get the tax rate for the various boroughs.

Why not two per cent or less. Because the interest and sinking fund charge on municipal debt and the State tax are not included in the *"Two per centum"* but are additional thereto. The limit for the interest and sinking fund charge as a fiscal burden is fixed in the *ten* per centum debt limit.

If a liability can be legally incurred, then the power to defray the interest and sinking fund charge thereon is presumed. And for that reason, interest and sinking fund charges were excluded from the 2 per cent tax limit. The only safeguard that the taxpayer has at present against an excessive interest and sinking fund charge is contained in the restriction of the debt-incurring power to 10 per cent of the assessed value of the real estate. The actual purpose of that restriction is to limit the interest and sinking fund charge as a tax burden. Therefore, no restriction for it was necessary in and through the 2 per cent tax limit.

Because of this fact, the last sentence in the paragraph quoted above from the transit study of this civic organization is without any basis in fact. Interest and sinking fund charges are not included in the two per cent tax restriction of the constitution but are a permitted burden additional to the two per centum to which local taxes are restricted.

Because this is the case the writer is suggesting in

this study of transit that the principle of a self-sustaining fare be embodied in the constitution of the State so that the actual and necessary cost of carrying a passenger shall be included in the fare. But he would restrict the fare to the actual and necessary cost because it is an inequitable method of levying what in effect is a tax and should be borne by the community as a tax—the sinking fund charge, if any, and deficits on new lines until traffic is developed to capacity.

It appears to the writer that the two per centum tax limit provision of the Constitution should be modified so that it will include interest and sinking fund charges on revenue producing investments so as to curb the urge to provide everybody with a subway at his door. That will make exemption of subway bonds from the constitutional debt limit less attractive and provide additional protection to the taxpayer. Owing to the preponderance of non-taxpayers in the voting population of a large city this additional curb on the taxing power seems to be needed. Deficits during the period in which traffic develops on a new subway are a proper charge to taxes. To include it in the two per cent tax limit will force giving correct principles vogue in the planning of additional subways.

CHAPTER VIII.

SINKING FUND — ORIGIN AND JUSTIFICATION

Through a sinking fund, while it accrues, the traveling public of the generation during which it accumulates taxes itself to give a present to future generations of subways for the construction and equipment of which the bonds were issued.

It is a moot question whether this burden additional to the burden of transit should be imposed on the traveling public of the present generation. It would appear that all that is ethically required of one generation is that a facility or mechanism of transit be kept in a high state of efficiency and be transferred to the following generation either unimpaired or with a reserve sufficient to cover any obsolescenc that may have occurred.

This merely requires a sufficient charge to operating expenses for a depreciation reserve so that it will permit replacement of worn out facilities as they occur, or contributing an amount equal to its cost if a more suitable facility is to be substituted.

Invention of labor saving devices is a continuing process. As a result, each succeeding generation can make a living with less effort or a better living with no more effort than the generation which precedes it. Because of this fact, the legally required sinking fund charge of today to operating expenses for investments in subways is ethically indefensible.

Sociologically, each generation should bear its own burden in all that pertains to earning a living. The cost of carrying a passenger is a part of that burden. By abolishing the sinking fund as a compulsory charge to income it will probably be possible to carry a passenger for nearly one (1) cent less a ride on the recapturable lines, and approximately a cent less per ride on subways constructed and equipped at the prevailing price of material and cost of labor, or at an average of nearly a cent less a ride.

It is not likely that the present price of material and cost of labor is permanent. When gold, the coin of which is our measure of value, is again the universal measure of value, our excess gold will have been shunted to countries not now on a gold basis. This wider distribution of gold will be the forerunner of a fall in the price of materials and cost of labor.

In its early history, the City issued Bonds almost exclusively for non-revenue producing improvements. Cancellation of such bonds was only possible through a sinking fund accumulated from annual charges to taxes.

In this way, amortization through a sinking fund became the habitual way of looking at municipal liabilities. With the extensive use of municipal credit in revenue producing enterprises, re-examination of the traditional way of regarding the sinking fund as a necessary method of cancelling municipal liabilities appears to be necessary.

Thus viewed, if a property for which the credit instrument is issued is kept in a good condition of repair, with an adequate reserve for obsolescence, a sinking fund, if a burden, seems to be unwarranted. A clear distinction should be drawn between municipal liabilities incurred for non-productive and for income producing properties. The former should be cancelled through the accumulation of a sinking fund, while in the case of the latter, the sinking fund charge may at least be waived during a period such as the present when the price of material and cost of labor are abnormally high and bid fair to be on a lower level a decade or more hence.

The sinking fund charge under Contract No. 1 and Contract No. 2 was negligible, in short, was so small that the then traditional five-cent fare covered it. It became a factor under Contract No. 3 and Contract No. 4, but it has been continued as the result of inertia. During the readjustment period, at least, the sinking fund on investments in rapid transit facilities should be abandoned because of its burdensome character.

Clearly the tradition that a sinking fund must attach to a municipal liability needs modification when the liability is incurred for an income producing enterprise that should and can be kept self-sustaining. Owing to the large item that the sinking fund charge will be for liabilities incurred for subways constructed and equipped at the prevailing price of material and cost of labor—nearly a cent a ride, it appears that the reason for modification or abandonment is compelling.

The sinking fund charge will henceforth be an important item of costs, because new subways must be constructed and equipped out of funds furnished by the City. There is no sentiment in favor of a return to private enterprise. The facilities themselves cannot remain half privately owned and half owned by the City. The objects and interests of the companies and of the City are too diverse. To the City a deficit is charged to taxes which is merely another way of paying for part of the burden of transit. To private owners, deficits mean insolvency. Two such necessarily diverse policies, human nature being what it is, cannot be successfully coordinated.

From this we are compelled to conclude that there must be complete municipal ownership and protection for transit bond holders by a constitutional guarantee that the securities of the enterprise will be kept self-sustaining. In order to ensure this, they must be given a 50 per cent voice in the direction of the enterprise, thus blending private operating efficiency with the low rate of interest of the City. This (municipal ownership of all rapid transit facilities) multiplies the importance of the sinking fund. The great cost of constructing and equipping subways at the prevailing price of material and cost of labor further adds to its magnitude.

Instead of being an unimportant item of the charge for transit as in the beginning of the City's subway venture, it may now be higher than 20 per cent of the operating revenue at a five-cent fare—as on the announced sections of the proposed municipal system. Its charge at the present rate, additional to that of the high cost of construction and equipment makes it a burden such that its continuance in its present form is probably politically impossible.

There is no inherent reason why amortization of a subway liability through a sinking fund should be compassed in 40 years rather than in 100 years. We appear to be in the peak of prices at present. Hence, it would appear that modification of the sinking fund charge is not only warranted but demanded by the exigencies of the situation, political and financial, and that provision for it should at least be deferred.

A sinking fund for transit bonds is merely a guarantee that there will be included in taxes if not paid out of income an amount that is sufficient to amortize the issue at maturity. Municipal guarantee of self-sustaining transit bonds requires that a fare be maintained that will cover the interest under normal traffic conditions and that there will be at maturity property of the same utility as the property for which the liability was incurred and a sinking fund in process of accumulation, that is, the provision for a sinking fund on the bonds outstanding as of the date when the plan becomes operative.

The two combined are a better guaranteee to the security holder and give greater marketability to a security than a sinking fund sufficient to amortize it at maturity without a guarantee that the fare will be self-sutaining, because a self-sustaining fare is evidence of correct municipal financiering. It is easier to re-issue an issue of transit bonds, or a part of an issue, than to float it in the first instance if the enterprise is properly managed and a self-sustaining fare is evidence of it.

When a plant or a facility has become obsolete, the depreciation reserve should have a credit balance equal in amount to its cost less salvage as the result of a constitutional requirement. If a sinking fund is provided in addition thereto as at present, there will be in it also an amount equal to cost. That is, future generations will get not only the cost of a plant through the plant itself plus the depreciation reserve but will also get its cost through a sinking fund; in short, will get the property as good as new or its equivalent and a sinking fund with which to pay for it.

A sinking fund for a non-revenue producing improvement other than land is the equivalent of a depreciation reserve for a self-sustaining income producing property. The protection for securities issued for their acquisition is the same. If in addition to an adequate depreciation reserve for a self-sustaining revenue producing property there is provided a sinking fund in being its security is greater than that of a municipal issue for a non-income producing property with merely a sinking fund to amortize it.

Assume $100,000,000 invested in subway equipment that lasts 38 years. Assume that transit bonds are issued therefor to mature at the same time and in the mortgage provision is made for their retirement at maturity through a sinking fund. At the end of the 38th year there will be $100,000,000 in the depreciation investment account less salvage and $100,000,000 in the sinking fund investment account. One of these items pays the debt. The other is a present to that and the next generation. There is no justification for a sinking fund if the security is issued for a self-sustaining revenue producing enterprise. In short, the straphanger pays for it twice—once through a charge to revenue for the depreciation reserve and the depreciation investment account and a second time through a charge to revenue for the sinking fund reserve and the sinking fund investment account.

In respect to subway liabilities, the City should take a leaf out of the notebook of corporation finance and, in so doing, develop the principle that debt may be quasi-permanent and can be employed by it for the purpose of securing capital at a low rate of interest in a field where private enterprise is moribund and, if properly safeguarded, is correct municipal financiering. If employed by a city it merely requires an adequate charge to operating expenses for renewals and replacements.

In an address before the Union League Club, Brooklyn, Commissioner Harkness made observations which indicate abandonment of the Transit Commission readjustment plan for the present and at the same time, he urged increase of the debt-incurring power for subways outside of the constitutional debt limit but available only for new construction.

It is the Craig plan severely edited just as the solution suggested herein is that of Mayor Hylan and of the Transit Commission adapted to existing conditions. The modified Craig plan preserves the five-cent fare as a political issue while the modified plan urged herein writes a self-sustaining fare into the constitutional structure of the State and clothes the revolving fund with a sanction. This plan is not revolutionary. The sinking fund goes on. Amounts now in its investment account will remain therein and will increase annually by interest accruals thereon. It accumulates as heretofore only at a different rate than if there were fixed annual contributions thereto from income or taxes on all the bonds outstanding.

At the maturity of the liability, there will be an asset of equal utility (value in use) and, in addition thereto, a sinking fund in process of accumulation, the two combined making a greater asset than the assets for which the liabilities were incurred.

The sinking fund is not a proper charge to revenue as it is not a part of the cost of carrying a passenger but rather should be charged to taxes if the community desires to amortize transit liabilities as at present.

Amortization through taxes would make it a collective burden. When amortized the transit system is collectively owned without a liability. This is the procedure in the case of non-revenue producing improvements. True, there is no other way in which the liability for a non-revenue producing improvement could be amortized. Both the revenue producing enterprise and the non-revenue producing improvement become community possessions and should be a community burden if the community desires to amortize subway liabilities as at present through a fixed annual contribution to a sinking fund.

Should title to all privately owned rapid transit facilities be vested in the City through a municipally owned corporation and through it the funds become available for the construction and equipment of the lines urgently needed, the City would own a rapid transit system worth from $1,200,000,000 to $1,600,000,000 by 1932.

We will assume that at that time it will be as good as new. It is a probability amounting to a certainty that its cost to reproduce less depreciation would be greater than this amount. If it is to be amortized through a sinking fund, the charge therefor will be from $12,000,000 to $16,000,000 annually. At the end of the amortization period the denizens of the then City will be the possessors of a transit system having the same value in use as it had when acquired and the assets to pay for the liability incurred to pay for it. A present of from $1,200,000,000 to $1,600,000,000 for which the straphangers paid. But that is not all. We will assume that deferred construction due to conflict over the mode of operation will have been made up by 1932. If, after that time, traffic increases at the rate in which it has increased since 1918, and if at that time the price level is still substantially the same as today, approximately $75,000,000 will be required annually for construction and equipment of additional subways.

That will require an additional $750,000 charge to revenue annually (in addition to the $12,000,000 to $16,000,000) for the sinking fund. Year in and year out, another $750,000 for the sinking fund as long as traffic grows at the current rate. In ten years there will be $7,500,000 additional to the $12,000,000 to $16,000,000, the amount growing as the traffic increases and as the years roll by. And for what purpose—for a present to future generations. Shall such a policy be continued?

If this is a proper procedure for a transit system, why not for a gas system, and, if for a gas system, why not for an electric lighting system, and, if for an electric lighting system, why not for a telephone system? It is the road to socialism through a process of evolution. It would appear self-evident that each generation is merely required to provide for obsolescence through an adequate charge to revenue for depreciation.

In other chapters, we have shown that a five-cent fare will cover the cost of carrying a passenger on the existing rapid transit lines if the sinking fund is eliminated as a compulsory charge to transit income, if equipment is provided at the low rate of interest charged the City. Modification of the sinking fund provision of the State Constitution as suggested in this analysis will make maintenance of the five-cent fare possible.

The sinking fund is not an actual and necessary part of the cost of carrying a passenger, and, therefore, is not properly includible in the fare. If the group or community desires to continue it in its present form, then it should be included in taxes. In theory, taxes should be levied according to ability to pay. By including the sinking fund in taxes the well-to-do section of the community will have to bear their proper proportion of this burden.

It certainly should be lifted from the straphanger. If it is included in taxes, he will bear materially less through shifting of it by the taxpayer to the rentpayer than he will bear if it is continued in the fare. Further, to continue it in the fare is abhorrrent to elementary principles of taxation.

In this chapter, we merely apply a fundamental, ethical principle, and, in so doing, show that the present day policy of including the sinking fund as a charge to transit income is at variance with social justice. It is immaterial whether the charge is on the $1,200,000,000 to $1,600,000,000 and on the $75,000,000 used for purposes of illustration, or on a lesser amount. These figures stand for an undefined but large amount. At this point we are not concerned with the amount but whether the amount, whatever it is, is a proper charge to transit income. Our analysis shows that the charge is highly improper.

Let us view the situation from a long period angle. Assume that the sinking fund on all outstanding subway bonds issued by the City up to the time that the unified rapid transit system becomes operative is continued as a charge to taxes. It will then apply to approximately $500,000,000 subway bonds. That amount of subway bonds would be amortized in about 40 years.

The interest that would accrue on that principal thereafter had there been no amortization, if set aside as a sinking fund, would amortize another $500,000,000 in about 18 years from that date; similarly the interest that would accrue on the then amortized $1,000,000,000 would amortize another billion in an additional 18 years. The amount amortized would be not less than $4,000,000,000 in a century. Clearly the sinking fund should be abandoned for subway bonds issued as of the date that the municipally owned, city-wide, five-borough rapid transit system is translated into a going concern.

This analysis shows that the revolving fund provision in the constitution of the State exempting self-sustaining transit bonds from the ten (10) per cent debt limit should not become inoperative if the sinking fund is excluded as a charge to transit income. To eliminate it as such a charge in computations to determine whether subway bonds are self-sustaining will require amendment of the constitution.

CHAPTER IX.

OTHER ADDITIONS TO NET INCOME

The foregoing amendments will effect a saving of about $10,000,000. Further installation of labor saving devices—pneumatic doors and adequate repair and inspection shops—will result in additional savings of about $3,000,000. As there is no tax on municipally owned enterprises, taxes will be eliminated, thereby reducing costs another $4,000,000. Growth in traffic will amount to more than 200,000,000 fare passengers between June 30, 1923, and January 1, 1928. That will mean more than $10,000,000 additional revenue of which less than 50 per cent will be absorbed by costs leaving more than $5,000,000 profit on this additional section or volume of business. The total of these items as they converge on January 1, 1928, is approximately $22,000,000.

As an offset, there is a deficit of approximately $13,-500,000 under the preferential system of revenue distribution as of June 30, 1923. Thereto must be added some $2,300,000 annually for depreciation. Other economies such as decrease in general expenses and saving in the cost of power will more than cover any deficiency in the amount allowed for depreciation should it prove inadequate. This leaves the $4,200,000 deficit on the Manhattan Railway under the preferential system, making a total of $20,000,000, leaving a surplus in excess of $2,000,000. It is a probability amounting to almost a certainty that in the process of the supersession of the stock of the three companies affected a very substantial saving in income deductions can be effected.

But, in addition to the foregoing, traffic will continue to grow and less than 50 per cent of the revenue that it yields will be absorbed by costs. It is thus clear that a substantial reserve can be accumulated before the process is arrested by the inclusion of subways constructed and equipped at the prevailing price of material and cost of labor. But to compass this end, modification of the sinking fund charge and reduction of the interest charge is necessary. Under this program the entire investment of the City under Contract No. 3 and Contract No. 4 will become self-sustaining, after January 1, 1928, and thereupon any unused balance can be declared exempt from the constitutional debt limit, giving the debt-incurring power needed for the construction of the urgently needed new subways.

Will the growth in net income resulting from additional traffic be permanent? Will additional facilities accommodate the excess traffic of today and the growth in traffic at a sufficiently reduced cost so that the profit on the additional volume of traffic will equal the amount in traffic at a sufficiently reduced cost so that the profit included in our program? President Menden of the B. M. T. testified at the transit hearing conducted by Judge McAvoy that if its subway station platforms are lengthened by the City and if the City fulfills its requirements under Contract No. 4, the carrying capacity of its lines would be doubled. President Hedley of the I. R. T. testified at the Transit Commission hearing on the lengthening of its local subway station platforms that if they are lengthened so that they will accommodate ten-car trains instead of six-car trains as now, its carrying capacity would be increased 33 per cent. In both cases the cost will be a mere bagatelle compared with the existing outlay for carrying a corresponding amount of traffic. The interest and sinking fund charge on the cost of these additional facilities will be almost negligible when compared with what it is for the facilities of a corresponding amount of the heretofore traffic on the existing lines or what it will be on the ensemble of traffic on new lines. The net income resulting from revenue due to the proposed additional facilities less expenses and other deductions will exceed the profit from growth in traffic used in the program. Therefore, this addition to net income will be permanent.

CHAPTER X.

DEBT-INCURRING POWER AD INTERIM

There was available $108,000,000 debt-incurring power as of March 1, 1925. The accruals from debt cancellation will be $36,740,000 in 1926 and $37,950,000 in 1927. Between January 1, 1926, and January 1, 1928, there can be made available over $100,000,000 from self-sustaining investment bonds under Contract No. 1, Contract No. 2, Contract No. 3 and Contract No. 4 in addition to annual accruals of perhaps $50,000,000 from increase in the assessment roll.

This can be effected by agreement between the operating companies and public officials authorized so to do to issue securities at their actuarial value for the unearned preferentials. This done, there will be a substantial surplus under Contract No. 3 by January 1, 1926, and an additional amount under it and a substantial amount under Contract No. 4 during 1927. In short, debt-incurring power in the amount needed for subway construction and the construction of additional school buildings can be made available during 1926 and 1927, if there is an intelligent will to arrange it. As already noted, if the constitutional amendments herein suggested are adopted, the entire investment under Contract No. 3 and Contract No. 4 will become self-sustaining after the enabling legislation has been enacted and the municipally owned and semi-municipally operated transit system has become operative as of January 1, 1928, or as soon thereafter as practicable.

This way out of the dilemma is made possible before all the economies noted in the previous chapter are made operative, because of the excessive density of traffic which is in process of becoming such as to require a legal enactment, "staggering of the peak," that is, spreading out the morning and evening rush hour traffic over a longer period by fixing the time of opening and closing of allied enterprises.

The additional traffic that could be carried as a result of such legislation would be carried through the same tubes and over the same viaducts and a much less per cent of the operating revenue would be absorbed by operating expenses and by interest and sinking fund charges as there would be no additional interest and sinking fund charge for tubes and viaducts.

This plan could not be put into effect, *de jure,* until January 1, 1928. *De facto* it could be put into effect as far as agreeing on terms is concerned as soon as it can be arranged between the City and the operating companies so that the unearned preferentials may be extinguished through supersession by another asset and, as a result effect a release of more than $100,000,000 of Contract No. 3 and of the Contract No. 4 investment from the constitutional debt limit for use in subway construction during 1926 and 1927.

The communication of Mr. Quackenbush for the I. R. T. to Judge McAvoy sitting as Moreland Act Commissioner warrants the conclusion that the above program can be translated into performance if there is an intelligent will to further subway construction.

The constitutional amendment proposed by Comptroller Craig will not make additional debt-incurring power available until 1928. The program formulated herein, if adopted, will make over $100,000,000 additional debt-incurring power available during 1926 and 1927.

Additional debt-incurring power may be made available by another method. Serial bonds in the amount needed may be issued in 1926 and 1927, maturing in annual instalments from 1929 to and including 1933 if a provision in the report of the Board of Transportation correctly interprets the authority of the City to incur debt to be liquidated through annual charges to taxes. To which may be added—if expected authority to liquidate through issue of long term bonds should not materialize. Before the time for their maturity arrives the investment of the City under Contract No. 3 and Contract No. 4 will become self-sustaining if the system proposed herein is adopted and debt-incurring power released in this way can be used to liquidate the aforementioned serial bonds as they mature without resort to taxation.

It is possible that the privately owned facilities and rights of the companies cannot be acquired at their fair value. Therefore, in order not to give the companies a strategic advantage as bargainers steps should be taken to liberalize the debt-incurring power provision in the constitution along the line in which water supply bonds have been issued so that it can be made effective in time to liquidate the serial bonds noted in the previous paragraph through issue of long term municipal bonds should the method suggested herein fail.

CHAPTER XI.

WHO PAYS THE BILLS

Carrying passengers by rapid transit facilities is a business enterprise. In this enterprise the City and the two operating companies are co-partners. The City gets interest and sinking fund payment on its investment under Contract No. 3 and Contract No. 4 only after all accruals of the operating companies have been defrayed from revenue. If revenue is insufficient excess costs accrue under unearned preferential accounts for both the City and the operating companies. Revenue has been insufficient to cover costs since Contract No. 3 and Contract No. 4 became operative. It is becoming adequate to cover all accruals of the operating companies owing to excessive density of traffic and economies effected through the installation of labor-saving devices. Growth in revenue, however, will not be sufficient to reduce the unearned preferentials of the City. This being so, who pays the deficits in the operation of the city-owned subways? Unearned preferentials and the contractual provision for their liquidation tell the story.

Insofar as revenue does not cover costs the burden is borne by the taxpayers to the extent that it is not shifted to the rentpayers. The same is true if needless burdens are unwisely placed upon the operating companies. Let us visualize the foregoing conclusions. Who pays deficits if revenue does not cover costs? The taxpayers and the rentpayers. Who pays additions to deficits caused by unwise regulation? The taxpayers and rent-payers. Who pays the bills if the companies have illegal regulatory orders set aside by due process of law? The taxpayers and rentpayers. Who pays for the destruction of the credit of the operating companies so that they must pay seven (7) per cent interest on loans instead of five (5) per cent? The taxpayers and rentpayers. Who pays for every unwise burden imposed upon the operating companies? The taxpayers and the rentpayers with a per cent added thereto by the taxpayers in the process of shifting the amount actually shifted to the rentpayers.

The preferential system of revenue distribution embodied in Contract No. 3 and Contract No. 4 enables us to state this conclusion in a formula: The taxpayers pay for deficits in the operation of city-owned subways howsoever caused to the extent that it is not shifted to the rentpayers.

It is thus apparent that every blow aimed at the operating companies due to the nature of Contract No. 3 and Contract No. 4 is a boomerang—injures the City and not the companies due to their co-partnership in an enterprise in which the City gets interest and sinking fund payments only after all the claims of the companies have been deducted from income. Therefore, if supervision is intelligent, it will be friendly in character so that the time may come or may be hastened when the City will get interest and sinking fund payment on its investment. Unfriendly regulation is subject to judicial review and, if found unreasonable, will be set aside as unconstitutional.

In the long run, taxpayers and rentpayers bear the burden, if fare passengers are carried below cost, as now over $10,000,000 of interest and sinking fund accruals on the City's investment under Contract No. 3 and Contract No. 4 are defrayed by taxes. As commuters and tourists fares are mounting toward 600, 000,000 annually according to the consulting engineer of the Transit Commission, a large non-resident traffic is carried at less than cost. Taxpayers and rentpayers not using rapid transit lines also pay for part of the transit burden of local passengers using subways. As no offsetting municipal benefit results from carrying non-resident passengers at less than cost it is an unwise policy from the standpoint of municipal finance.

Both operating companies are now in a position to meet all contractual obligations as they arise. Growth in traffic and operating economies in process of installation will increase net corporate income to such an extent that there will be a safe margin for contingencies. Contrast this with the acute financial embarrassment of the City and couple it with the slow but sure pressure of the law of costs and it will become clear that a fare that will cover costs may be delayed at the exepense of the taxpayers and rentpayers but cannot be prevented.

Taxes in New York City are largely paid by those who own no property. They are shifted by property owners to the rentpayers. General O'Ryan expressed views which reinforce the foregoing in an address from which the following excerpt is taken:

> Practically all rent payers feel that rents are exorbitant and that the space and facilities they have are inadequate. But the first step in improving these conditions is for these people to realize that a very substantial percentage of the rentals they pay represents taxes paid into the City Treasury.

Of the same import are the views expressed by Mayor Hylan in his comments on mandatory legislation passed by the legislature. They are contained in the paragraph which follows:

> I regret very much that the Legislature put through mandatory legislation which places a burden of from $20,000,000 to $25,000,000 upon the taxpayers of New York City. The rent payers will find most of that burden shifted to them.

As already noted, a mandatory self-sustaining fare should be embodied in the constitutional structure of the State. If this is done and if a friendly supersession of existing securities is effected through exchange for municipally guaranteed transit bonds, then the public probably can be made to understand that carrying passengers is business, that it costs and the greater the comforts the greater the burden, that is, the higher the fare. It appears at present that this is the only way in which to stop the clamor for a parlor car service at a five cent fare.

CHAPTER XII.

ECONOMIC RENT IN THE TRANSIT SITUATION

Subways constructed and equipped at the prevailing price of material and cost of labor will have a high interest and sinking fund charge per single mile of track until the bonds issued therefore have been cancelled. That is approximately forty years after issue. Subways constructed and equipped under Contract No. 3 and Contract No. 4 have an appreciably lower interest and sinking fund charge than subways constructed at the prevailing price of material and cost of labor. The subways constructed under Contract No. 1 and Contract No. 2 have a very much lower interest and sinking fund charge than those constructed under Contract No. 3 and Contract No. 4 or than the average for those constructed under Contract No. 3, Contract No. 4 and those constructed at the prevailing price of material and cost of labor. The interest and sinking fund charge on the Manhattan elevated is less than that of Contract No. 1 and Contract No. 2 if the return on its existing capitalization is computed at the same rate. The interest and sinking fund charge of the Brooklyn elevated is the lowest of all and will be the lowest still after all parts that are required to be have been reconstructed so as to permit operation thereon of subway trains. The marked difference in the relatively permanent interest and sinking fund charges of the various rapid transit lines per single mile of track has created such a complicated situation that rare intelligence is needed to deal with it.

In Chapter XV. we will show that the interest and sinking fund charge on subways constructed at the prevailing price of material and cost of labor will probably be not less than $200,000 per single mile of track. Contract No. 3 and most of Contract No. 4 lines are recapturable. The permanent charges under these contracts will be approximately $60,000 less per single mile of track than on subways constructed at the prevailing price of material and cost of labor. Should these contracts be carried out as negotiated save that the fare is changed so as to cover the cost of carrying a passenger on extensions, the profits thereunder for distribution between the City and the companies on the 50-50 basis would be substantial . Contract No. 3, however, is merged with Contract No. 1 and Contract No. 2. After allowing for the profit item in the 8.76 per cent that the City gets on its investment under Contract No. 3 and a corresponding amount for the I. R. T. there would still remain a substantial profit for distribution annually on the 50-50 basis.

Next comes the Manhattan elevated operated by the I. R. T. The table which follows mirrors the situation:

Fixed Capital Per Single Mile of Track

Year Ending	*No. of Miles*	*Total fixed Capital*	*Per single mile of track*
June 30, 1913....	118	$111,445,908	$950,000
June 30, 1924....	123	151,000,000	1,100,000

It only operates seven-car trains. It is necessary to add nearly 100 per cent of the $1,100,000 to itself to equalize capitalization of its carrying capacity with the cost of the same amount of carrying capacity of the eight-car trains that will probably be operated on the new subways in process of construction — a new car having about 75 per cent more carrying capacity than an old car. That gives it a cost per single mile of track or unit of carrying capacity of a little more than $2,000,000 or a little more than 50 per cent of the same amount of carrying capacity of subways constructed at the prevailing price of material and cost of labor, which is, as we will show later, about $4,000,000 per single mile of track. In addition it must be noted that it has outstanding $45,000,000 long-term bonds at 4 per cent and no sinking fund charge thereon. Compare that with the 5 per cent or higher interest and sinking fund charge on the projected municipal system or on newly constructed subways at prevailing prices.

The above ratios are predicated on identical traffic conditions. But traffic conditions are not identical. The ensemble of traffic on the Manhattan elevated lines is of a shorter haul character than what that of the projected independent system will be. It has four trunk lines to only three feeder lines, while the I. R. T. subway subdivision has ten feeder line tracks to eight trunk line tracks and the new system appears to be modelled on the latter type rather than on that of the former. The higher percentage of trunk lines to feeder lines permits operation of all sections of the elevated nearer to capacity than those of the existing I. R. T. subways or than those of the projected new system. Approaching the subject from the standpoint of traffic, its carrying capacity per unit length is only about 33 1-3 per cent less than what that of the projected independent system will be—as $150,000 per single mile of track is to $225,000. These figures are for approximately the same density of traffic. Per unit of capitalization, the carrying capacity of the elevated is to that of the projected independent system as 4 is to 10; that is, for the same amount of carrying capacity there will be an interest and sinking fund charge on new subways on about $10 for every $4 on the Manhattan elevated. In other words, if financed on the same terms, the fixed charges for the same amount of carrying capacity would be about 150 per cent more on the projected system than on the elevated. Whatever advantage the new system will have in length of platform and hence in length of train is more than offset by the lesser capitalization of the elevated coupled with a more favorable percentage of short haul to long haul traffic and by a more favorable percentage of trunk lines to feeder lines, permitting all parts of the system to be operated nearer to capacity. Per unit of carrying capacity, under identical traffic conditions, the facilities of the Manhattan elevated are capitalized about 50 per cent less than what that of the independent system will be if engineering estimates are substantially correct.

The situation with reference to the Brooklyn elevated is at least as favorable to the company as that of the Manhattan elevated if not more so. It is more difficult to reduce its situation to figures because some of its track has been reconstructed and it is not operated as a separate financial agency. Note the figures in the table which follows:

FIXED CAPITAL PER SINGLE MILE OF TRACK

Year Ending	*No. of Miles*	*Total Fixed Capital*	*Per Single Mile of Track*
June 30, 1913....	123	$57,406,398	$470,000
June 30, 1924....	148	144,521,673	1,000,000

The company has outstanding underlying bonds, $16,-000,000 at 5 per cent and $7,000,000 at 4 per cent. Its new financing for the rapid transit lines is at five per cent plus 1 per cent for the sinking fund. Its position as to the permanent interest rate is somewhat higher than that of the City but that of the City will be on a materially larger investment for the same amount of carrying capacity.

The ratios for both elevated sections of the existing rapid transit facilities will be developed and amplified in Chapter XIV. In that chapter these facilities will be discussed from the standpoint of the capitalization of their carrying capacity when compared with that of the same unit of carrying capacity for subways constructed and equipped and the prevailing price of material and cost of labor.

Not only can a substantial part of the economic rent

items noted above be saved to the travelling public by municipal ownership of all rapid transit facilities and semi-municipal operation, but a more economical use can be made of the transit facilities through such a merger. Dead ends of lines in the heart of the City can be utilized through extensions into residential sections. Instance the B. M. T. Line up Broadway to 59th Street. By extending it to Washington Heights the tube through the business section of the City will have a two-way movement of traffic mornings and evenings instead of only a one-way movement in the morning and a movement in the opposite direction in the evening. Engineers will be able to apply the principle just instanced wherever possible in the event of the merger of all rapid transit lines as suggested in this analysis.

In private enterprise profit is the lure. Owing to the great extent economic rent is now a factor in the transit situation, it seems to be necessary to substitute operation at cost for operation at a profit. This requires that the interest on investments be guaranteed through a self-sustaining fare so that revenue will always cover the cost of carrying a passenger. That will make rapid transit bonds as safe investments as bonds of the City. The plan mirrored herein, provides for coupling the low interest rate of the City with the operating efficiency of private enterprise. Experience shows that when the City pays 3½ per cent interest, operating companies pay about five (5) per cent. On $400,000,000, which is approximately the amount of the funded lien on the rapid transit facilities or income, the saving in interest alone may be not less than $4,000,000 a year. This would be additional to the saving resulting from socializing as much as possible of the economic rent shown in this chapter.

There must be added to the above noted differentials (economic rent), the fact that the bonds of the I. R. T. will be amortized through a sinking fund as of December 31, 1956. Its contracts with the City do not expire until December 31, 1967. As a result there will be no charge against the $6,335,000 and none against the $4,800,000 interest charge on the $80,000,000 specified contribution of the company to construction and equipment. That amounts to $11,135,000 for a period of eleven (11) years or $122,485,000. This amount, too, can be saved to the then public if the transit situation is intelligently handled and not as the football of politics.

The foregoing was almost entirely written before the investigation of the transit situation by Judge McAvoy as a Moreland Act Commissioner. The views expressed herein so far, were confirmed by testimony given at the hearing on pre-war and post-war costs of construction—the latter being about 125 per cent greater than the former. Note the following observations taken from this testimony:

> Would you mind asking how much the cost per mile of construction of this new validated line will be if the Commissioner can give the figures? Judge Shearn said to Mr. Sherman and the latter put the desired question.

I will give you the figures, said Mr. Delaney. The mileage included in the recently adopted routes that are not yet validated is ten miles and the mileage of the previously adopted routes is 6.65 miles. That portion which will go to the yard is about a mile, so that you would have at that rate about 17.65 miles. The estimated cost with yards, real estate and construction is $188,457,000. Now, if some one will kindly make that calculation you will get the average. The estimates are not made that way, of course.

Mr. Sherman announced that an assistant had made the calculation, which showed about $10,600,000 a mile. How could that be made to compare with the cost per mile of construction under Contract 3? asked Judge Shearn.

My recollection is that the estimate of construction for these subway lines, track for track and under certain conditions, will cost nearly, if not quite, double what the construction was at least in the early days of Contract No. 3 [and Contract No. 4] Mr. Delaney replied. The costs of labor and material are almost as high as they were immediately after the war.

And that road, that is to cost twice as much per mile, is to be operated on a 5-cent fare? asked Judge Shearn.

Well, we will not go into that for the moment, said Mr. Sherman. It would be operated according to the law—whatever the law may say on that subject, I assume.

Whatever the law says, of course, said Mr. Delaney.

MR. MOONEY: For your information, Mr. Sherman. Mr. Ridgeway (chief engineer of the Board of Transportation) has just said that the percentage would be about 125 per cent, in comparison.

MR. SHERMAN: More than double the former cost?

MR. RIDGWAY: Yes, costs have more than doubled. I am speaking of the cost today and the cost in pre-war times.

MR. DELANY: Mr. Ridgway has made an important qualification. Of course, a great part of Contract No. 3 was constructed during and after the war. So I think we may safely estimate that this new construction will cost nearly twice as much as the construction we had under Contract No. 3, taking into account that part of the former construction was done during these high-priced times also.

MR. SHERMAN: That is a very clear statement, sir. Let me see whether I apprehend it. Even taking the costs under Contract No. 3 and Contract No. 4, as they were swollen during war times for such part as was constructed during war times, taking the entire total there and comparing it with the total per mile cost today, the relation would be about 125 per cent higher than the costs that were actually incurred in the construction per mile of Contracts Nos. 3 and 4?

MR. DELANY: I am afraid that must be nearly so.

Let us apply this testimony as to costs to the rapid transit systems enumerated herein. It costs nearly twice as much per mile of track to construct and equip subways today as that of Contract No. 3 and Contract No. 4; more than twice as much as that of Contract No. 1 and Contract No. 2; and similarly, almost four times as much as that of the Manhattan elevated and the Brooklyn elevated. Contract No. 3 and most of Contract No. 4 are recapturable; the economic rent on the non-recapturable and privately owned lines will be approximately 100 per cent and 150 per cent respectively of the interest and sinking fund charge of new lines per unit of carrying capacity after station platforms for Contract No. 1 and Contract No. 2 lines have been lengthened. This is mute evidence that all rapid transit lines should be merged into a municipally-owned system and be operated by a non-political agency.

Recapture of Contract No. 3 and Contract No. 4 lines if it were practicable and merging them into an independent system with new lines constructed as extensions would be no remedy as the difference between its interest and sinking fund charge and that of the company-owned elevated and the non-recapturable Contract No. 1 and Contract No. 2 lines is prohibitive. A higher fare on the new system would mean that five (5) cent fare lines would have nearly all of the non-rush hour and more than their share of the rush hour traffic where an alternative route is possible and that would be the case in much of Manhattan and in much of Brooklyn and the Bronx.

Viewing the economic factors in the light of present day political necessity it appears that the way out of a situation that is in process of becoming a tragedy is operation at cost. That appears to be possible only under complete municipal ownership and semi-municipal or non-political operation. In the preface and an earlier chapter we stated that the fair value of the privately owned and non-recapturable rapid transit lines is the actuarial value of the earnings, actual and potential, of the companies for their securities in contracts with the City.

CHAPTER XIII.

RECAPTURE PROVISIONS IN THE DUAL CONTRACTS

The recapture provisions in the Dual Contracts should be thoroughly understood as it is the announced policy of the City to exercise it, as soon as practicable, after its accrual. It accrued for all the recapturable lines of Contract No. 4 on August 4, 1923, and it will accrue for all of Contract No. 3 Lines on June 22, 1925.

The recapture provisions are so drawn that it is a probability amounting to a certainty that the negotiators of these contracts intended merely to confer the power of recapture so that it could be exercised as part of a plan for municipal ownership of all rapid transit lines, and not as the present City administration intends to exercise it.

Note the lines of the rapid transit division of the B. M. T., that is, those of Contract No. 4 and of its elevated extension and reconstruction certificates. Those owned by the City and those owned by the company are such an integral part of a system that they could not be operated as a traffic unit and as separate financial agencies as is done under Contract No. 3 and its related elevated extension certificate. Reconstructed portions of company-owned lines serve as extensions of City-owned lines. There is no provision for acquisition of reconstructed company-owned lines by the City. There is, however, provision that some City-owned lines cannot be recaptured. Clearly recapture of Contract No. 4 lines is impracticable as segregation of the City-owned and the company-owned lines for purpose of operation would cause intolerable inconvenience to the travelling public.

There is another obstacle of moment. The City in the event of recapture pursuant to notice is required to give to the B. M. T. trackage rights over the Nassau-Broad Street line if the Broadway-Fourth Avenue line is recaptured. Construction of the Nassau-Broad Street line has been definitely abandoned by the City. It is not even the intention of the present City administration to construct it unless ordered to do so by the Court. Below is given the contract provisions relating to trackage rights on this line.

> The City . . . agrees in the event of the termination of the Contract as to the Broadway-Fourth Avenue Line . . . to grant to the lessee for a period equal to the then unexpired term of the contract (if it had not been so terminated) the right to use the tracks, structure and line equipment of the following portion of the Broadway-Fourth Avenue Line:
>
> Two tracks beginning at a point in the Borough of Manhattan near the intersection of South and Broad Streets, and extending thence under Broad Street and Nassau Street to Park Row and under Park Row to a point under the Municipal Building.

In addition thereto, when one considers the trackage

rights, transfer and reconstruction problems that it would create, one must conclude that recapture of City-owned lines by the City for municipal operation is impossible when viewed from the standpoint of operation. It would appear that recapture was incorporated in this contract in order to chloroform opposition. At least, the negotiators of this contract did not intend that it should be exercised peacemeal as the present City administration contemplates to exercise it if continued in power long enough to do so. Recapture of these lines is practicable only in connection with municipalization of the elevated lines also; that is, of all the B. M. T. rapid transit lines.

The recapture provisions of Contract No. 3 lines must be viewed from a slightly different angle. Contract No. 1 and Contract No. 2 contain no recapture clauses. They occupy the most lucrative rapid transit route on earth. They tap Times Square, Grand Central, Brooklyn Bridge and the Long Island Railroad terminal at Atlantic Avenue.

Contract No. 3 provides for the recapture of a continuous east or west side line but the exchange of parts necessary to make it possible is to be effected by compensation of difference in value and not on difference in cost of construction of equal units.

What is the difference in value? A fruitful field for litigation. Recapture is beset with additional difficulties. Transfer and reconstruction arrangements still further complicate it.

The elevated division of the I. R. T. is operated as a separate financial unit. This was made possible by permitting each unit to retain the money it collects. At connecting points there is freedom of transfer. Its capitalization per mile of single track is less than one third of what that of lines to be constructed and equipped at the prevailing price of material and cost of labor will be. Its traffic is largely short haul and in a section of the City where it is dense. How can the City with its operating inefficiency compete with efficiently operated open air lines?

According to Chairman McAneny recapture of Contract No. 3 and Contract No. 4 lines in connection with the projected independent system would mean that nearly 900,000 passengers would be compelled to ride on either two or three systems instead of one if all lines are merged into a single municipally owned and semi-municipally operated system and so would be compelled to pay either two or three fares each way, instead of a single fare as now. The observation from which the foregoing is a resume concludes as follows:

> There would be 327,000 such passengers now using the Interborough lines who would come in such a category, including the 125,000 persons who use the Forty-second Street shuttle daily to transfer between the East and West Side Interborough lines. On the B. M. T. system, because of the hooking up of many elevated lines in joint subway and 'L' operation, he said the number would be much greater and estimated it at 550,000 passengers a day.
>
> When the people of the City who use these lines realize that recapture means nothing more than a transfer of title for a huge consideration and that it means,

> incidentally, this multiplication of double fares, they are not going to stand for it for a moment. I venture that not merely as a prophecy, but it is so clearly the thinking habit of the traveler that he is in my judgment sure to come to that conclusion.

Clearly, the logic of the situation points to the merger of all rapid transit lines into a single municipally-owned system. In an earlier chapter we discussed municipal versus semi-municipal operation.

CHAPTER XIV.

SUPERSESSION OF THE ELEVATED LINES IN BUSINESS CENTERS

In another chapter we have shown that the revenue per single mile of track on the elevated division of the I. R. T. is $158,000. It can operate only seven-car trains. When this is converted into the six-ten-car train basis of the subway division of the I. R. T. it shows that the density of traffic on the "open-air" elevated line is greater than in the subways. From this it follows that the elevated lines have not lost favor as a transit facility. Hence the compensation that must be paid to the owner in event of removal by condemnation is not based on their value as junk but on their value as a desirable and efficient transit mechanism. This voids the "junk" part of the argument against the plan to which this analysis points. In short, as a higher fare is inevitable unless transit costs are drastically reduced and as it is highly probable that these lines can now be acquired cheaper under the municipal ownership and semi-municipal operation plan than later by condemnation, their early acquisition will hasten rather than retard creation of a city-wide transit system.

Let us view it from another angle. The Court of

Appeals has declared that an obligation or condition imposed by Contract No. 3 "has the force of a public statute." That is then equally true for the elevated extension and reconstruction certificates which are merely coordinate contracts of Contract No. 3 and Contract No. 4. In Consolidated Gas versus Wilcox the United States Supreme Court virtually held that capitalization once crystallized into a public statute is not revocable by a legal enactment. It appears from the foregoing that the capitalization of the elevated lines as of March 19, 1913 less retirements plus additions thereto since that date may be the lowest figure that would be awarded the owners in the event of removal by condemnation.

Removal by condemnation can only be justified on the basis of social necessity and not on account of obsolescence as a transit mechanism. Viewed from this anit appears that objection to the acquisition of the elevated lines on the ground that they are transit junk is due to a confusion of their usefulness as a means of transit with their unsightliness in the street, their blighting effect on real estate values and the need of the space occupied by them to relieve congestion of street traffic in business centers.

Chairman McAneny estimated the cost of renewing the Sixth Avenue Elevated through condemnation proceedings at approximately $12,000,000. That figure is in harmony with the foregoing analysis. Characterization of the elevated lines as traction junk is clearly without foundation. With the "traction junk" argument eliminated there remains no valid objection to the merger of all the rapid transit lines into a single unified system —municipally owned and semi-municipally operated.

The theory underlying the position of the City seems to indicate that the operating companies to which the subways are leased must bear the hardships due to the upheaval in the price level and the resulting inadequacy of the five-cent fare but must not be permitted to share in the benefit that accrued generally to property owners as a result of the rise in the price level. That brings us to a consideration of economic value. Value in use of property today is not original cost but cost to reproduce. Value in exchange is based on earnings—in the case of the rapid transit lines, earnings at a five-cent fare. The City apparently hopes to acquire the privately owned and non-recapturable rapid transit lines at original cost less depreciation with authority to operate. In order not to ease the burden of the operating companies, it foregoes making arrangements so that it will get interest and sinking fund payment on its investment under the Dual Contracts which will exceed $300,000,000 when all construction is completed. But the companies will earn their preferentials during the current fiscal year and are on the threshold of earning enough to amortize their unearned preferentials. Their properties have been properly maintained according to a report of disinterested transit engineers. These observations indicate that the City and the operating companies are deadlocked and that an endurance test is on.

As safeguarded as property rights are in our constitutional and legal structure, it is a probability amounting to a certainty that the program of the City in-so-far as it relates to the privately owned and non-recapturable rapid transit lines cannot be realized.

Under the original Transit Commission valuation, the 6th Avenue Elevated was appraised at slightly more than $5,000,000. We have already noted Chairman McAneny's estimate of the cost of its removal under condemnation proceedings. The forthcoming decision of Judge O'Malley concerning the removal of the 42nd Street spur after it has been passed upon by the Court of Appeals may show whether the elevated lines can be scrapped as junk, be removed at original cost less depreciation or on some other basis to ascertain fair value. Once the pending issues are legally settled, it is believed that the outcome will show that the elevated lines can now be acquired as cheap if not cheaper through negotiation than be removed later through condemnation proceedings. If so, then the formula given in the last paragraph of this chapter will ensure their elimination from business centers without cost to the City if they are now acquired at their fair value which is either the actuarial value of the earnings applicable for payment on their outstanding securities or at cost to reproduce less depreciation.

Let us examine obsolescence further. It means inability to function or ability to function only at such a disadvantage that supersession would be cheaper.

Judged by this criterion the Manhattan elevated railway is not removable at its value as scrap. It still has a greater carrying capacity per unit of capitalization than subways constructed and equipped at the prevailing price of material and cost of labor will have, and hence a greater revenue producing capacity per unit of capitalization. If municipally owned it would be free from taxes. There is no tax charge on city-owned subway property and in that respect the city would have an advantage but that would not be an inherent or business advantage nor even a fair competitive advantage. After all factors are properly weighted the earning capacity of the Manhattan Railway per unit of capitalization will still be greater than that of the projected city-owned system. The advantage that the I. R. T. has under Contract No. 1 and Contract No. 2 is as great and will more than offset any disadvantage that the Manhattan Railway is under due to taxes if deficits on city-owned and municipally operated lines are included in taxes. It will cost less to carry a passenger on it per unit of book cost than on up-to-date lines constructed and equipped at the prevailing price of materials and cost of labor. These observations have reference to operation under the existing legal structure.

From this it appears that acquisition of the Manhattan Railway is conscienable at cost to reproduce less depreciation or at the actuarial value of the earnings applicable to the outstanding securities of the company.

It is the intention of the City at this writing to recapture Contract No. 3 lines when new lines are ready for operation. If, and if, when this aim is realized the Manhattan Railway Company will have more revenue from the same volume of traffic due to abolition of the existing free transfer privilege. This will add to its exchange value. Acquisition through negotiation appears to be the most advantageous solution for the City.

As already noted in an earlier chapter, under the same traffic conditions, the Manhattan elevated has an advantage over new subways when viewed from the standpoint of capitalization in the ratio of nearly 5 to 10, that is, the same carrying capacity of the elevated under the same traffic conditions is capitalized at nearly 50 per cent less than what that of the new subways will apparently be. But when viewed from the standpoint of what the carrying capacity of the elevated actually is and what that of the new subways will be, the ratio is approximately that of 4 to 10, that is, the elevated will have an advantage of about 150 per cent over that of the projected new subways. Owing to its importance we will develop the ratio. The Manhattan elevated revenue per single mile of track was $158,000 for the fiscal year ended June 30, 1924. Increase that by 50 per cent and you will get the approximate maximum capacity of that of the projected system if completed along the line on which it is being planned. Now increase its present capitalization ($1,100,000 per single mile of track) by 50 per cent and you get approximately $1,650,000, while the cost of new subways will be approximately $4,000,000, or about 150 per cent more than the capitalization of the elevated for the same carrying capacity. The excess advantage over that noted above is due to more favorable traffic conditions. View the situation as you may, the actual capitalization of the Manhattan Railway Company per mile of single track is less than cost to reproduce, less depreciation and materially less than that of the same carrying capacity of the projected independent system—is apparently only as much as that of the cost of equipping a mile of new subway track.

In order to confirm the above ratio, we will develop it by a different method. We will take $150,000 as the revenue per single mile of track on the elevated and $225,000 as that of the projected independent system. At the capitalization of the elevated, $1,100,000, an investment of $7 1-3 will produce $1 in revenue. At the indicated capitalization of the new lines, $4,000,000, an investment of $18 2-3 will produce $1 in revenue. The advantage of the elevated over new subways is as 7 1-3 is to 18 2-3, that is, the same capitalization on the elevated will produce about 150 per cent more revenue.

In this analysis, so far specific reference has only been made to the elevated division of the I. R. T. due to the fact that it is operated as a separate financial agency. Not so with the elevated division of the B. M. T. It and Contract No. 4 lines are operated as a financial unit. If separate data were available they would probably show even more decisively that per unit of capitalization that the elevated division of the B. M. T. has a greater revenue-producing capacity than that of the subway system projected by the Board of Transportation. Therefore, the arguments that we have advanced so far against the claim that the Manhattan elevated lines are merely transit junk apply as well to the elevated division of the B. M. T. as to that of the I. R. T.

Much of the B. M. T. elevated has been reconstructed. That cost was nearly as much as new. It was largely done at a lower price level. Much of it was of an open-cut and the rest of a viaduct character and the cost thereof was from one-third to one-half that of subways. It has, however, the same traffic capacity per unit length. Its original capitalization was low as an appreciable part of it was on the surface—only $470,000 per single mile of track including equipment. Its present capitalization is only about $1,000,000 per single mile of track. These facts clearly show that per unit of carrying capacity the capitalization of the B. M. T. elevated is at least as much less than that of subways constructed and equipped at the prevailing price of material and cost of labor than is that of the Manhattan elevated.

Because of the five-cent fare provision contained in the Dual Contracts and in the elevated extension and reconstruction certificates the City can probably acquire more carrying capacity per unit of investment by it if it acquire through negotiation the privately owned elevated and non-recapturable subway lines than it gets in constructing and equipping new lines at the prevailing price of material and cost of labor. In short, the logic of the situation points to the merger of all rapid transit lines under municipal ownership and operation at cost through a non-political agency.

If the elevated lines are acquired under the plan herein proposed, it should be the declared policy of the City that whenever the owners of real estate along any line in the business center give tangible proof of willingness to pay the cost of the removal of an elevated line and pay the cost of the construction of an equal amount of underground carrying capacity, the City will proceed with its elimination, confident that the increase in the assessed value of the adjoining real estate resulting from removal of the elevated structure will give the additional debt-incurring power needed to pay for the balance of the cost of an underground line constructed as a substitute.

CHAPTER XV.

NEW SUBWAYS — A UNIFIED SYSTEM

The two preliminary reports of the Board of Transportation give vital facts bearing on the cost of carrying a passenger on new lines. With them other facts bearing on the situation can be computed. In these reports, 119 miles of additional subway track are outlined whose construction will cost approximately $3,200,000 per single mile. Equipment will cost approximately $1,000,000. This gives a total cost of about $4,200,000 per single mile of track for the sections of the system as far as outlined on March 20, 1925. Some of the routes not yet outlined will be open-cut and so will cost materially less per single mile of track. But it will be largely offset by the great cost of the tunnel under the Narrows to Staten Island. In the light of these observations, it is safe to assume that the average cost of the projected system will not fall materially below $4,000,000 per single mile of track.

The interest and Sinking Fund charge on this investment will probably be at the rate of 5 per cent or about $200,000 per single mile of track. Operating expenses will add approximately $125,000 thereto if we include interest on working capital and an adequate charge for depreciation. This gives a cost of about $325,000 to operate a single mile of track. It is a moot question whether operating revenues will materially exceed $225,000 per single mile of track without undue crowding after traffic has been developed to capacity on the system as roughly outlined. These figures indicate that the actual cost of carrying a passenger under existing conditions will be more than five cents for a single ride even if the system is operated by the City as efficiently as are those of the present operating companies. It is a probability amounting to a certainty that it will not be as efficiently operated.

It is believed that the figure used for operating expenses is adequate if the system is operated through a non-political agency. The sinking fund charge, if excluded, will reduce fixed charges approximately $40,000 per single mile of track. It amounts to nearly one cent per ride. The figures given so far are representative. They indicate that a five-cent fare will not cover the actual and necessary cost of carrying a passenger on lines constructed, equipped and operated at the prevailing price of material and cost of labor unless properly planned. We will give data from official reports and therewith develop the above figures and, in so doing, show that our conclusions are statistically warranted.

We did not alter the manuscript to conform to the final Report of the Board of Transportation as the data culled from the earliest reports is probably more representative of what the cost per single mile of track will finally be than the latest figures.

If *eight* car trains on a system have double the revenue producing capacity of *four* car trains, then there is no inherent reason why the equivalent of *twelve* car trains should not have treble the revenue producing capacity. The local trains on the subway division of the I. R. T. have six cars and the express trains have ten cars during the rush period, which is an average of *eight* car trains for the local and express tracks combined. On the new mileage, trains of the length of twelve I. R. T. cars may be operated during rush hours if tentative plans are translated into reality. In addition thereto these cars will be ten feet wide. Those of the I. R. T. are only nine feet wide.

A car of the B. M. T. type has 45 per cent more floor space than a car of the I. R. T. type. Its seating arrangements are such that a car has 62½ per cent more seating capacity than an I. R. T. car. But a passenger on a seat with that seat occupies nearly twice the space of a straphanger. The relation of the seats to the exits of the B. M. T. cars are such that it is a moot question whether B. M. T. cars will accommodate more passengers during rush hour than I. R. T. cars. It appears to the writer that a ten-car I. R. T. train will accommodate at least as many and probably more passengers than an eight car train on the projected lines.

The data used for computing the carrying capacity of the new subways are taken from the testimony of Mr. Ridgway, Chief Engineer of the Board of Transportation at the transit hearing conducted by Judge McAvoy—minutes, pages 1925 and 1926, supplemented by inspection of cars in operation. The testimony of Mr. Ridgway is of controlling importance in this analysis. Therefore, vital excerpts therefrom are given below:

> The stations that we are designing are for twelve car Interborough trains; at least, the equivalant length of that. . . . When the original subways were designed, they had a nine-foot wide car on the Interborough system. The new subways are designed for a ten-foot wide car. . . .
>
> The Interborough cars being approximately 51 feet long and the B. M. T. cars being 67 feet long, with longer overhang from the trucks, so that in negotiating curves it is necessary to have a greater width of structure to accommodate those cars, and provision is made in the new plans for such a car so that such a car can operate through the new subways.

From this it appears that on the new lines as now projected nine car trains of the B. M. T. type of car can be operated. It is a moot question whether such a train will accommodate more passengers during the rush hour than a ten-car train on the I. R. T. subways. It seems to us, other factors being equal, that the revenue producing capacity of a new B. M. T. train will not be greater than that of an I. R. T. train. As the B. M. T. asked for eight-car length stations, we will use that figure in our further analysis.

Other factors enter into the revenue producing capacity of a single mile of track, that is, such as the length of haul and the proportion of feeder to trunk line tracks. If new trunk lines are properly articulated with new and existing feeder line tracks so that traffic will tax both to capacity revenue per single mile of track will be greater than the $225,000 used in Chapter IV. If the new feeder lines are planned so as to limit the length of the haul and if the proportion of short-haul to long-haul traffic is increased revenue per single mile of track will be greater still. This line of reasoning points to the fact that if you cannot increase the fare you can decrease the cost of carrying a passenger by judicious planning.

We have already referred to the preliminary reports of the Board of Transportation. The statistical summaries which accompanied the second report are so vital a part of the analysis contained in this chapter that we include them in their entirety. Below we give their contents with their form adapted to the printed page.

A complete tabulation of the routes adopted by the Board of Transportation last December, with revised estimates of cost due to changes in track mileage for operation, appended to its second report is as follows:

Route	*Est. Cost*	*Route Miles*	*Track Miles*
Wall St., East River to Thames St.	$8,000,000	.75	1.50
Church St., Thames to Lispenard St...	7,881,000	.86	1.72
Sixth Ave., Lispenard to Carmine St...	6,143,000	.74	1.88
Sixth Ave., Carmine St. to 53rd St.....	23,082,000	2.47	7.74
Eighth Av., 64th St. to Eighth St.......	34,527,000	2.95	11.80
53rd St., East River to Eighth Av.....	16,582,000	1.70	5.82
Houston St., Carmine St. to Bowery....	3,531,000	.70	1.40
Central Park West, 64th to 108th St...	21,592,000	2.20	8.80
Cen'tl P'k W., 8th Av., 108th to 124th..	7,400,000	.80	3.20
St. Nicholas Av., 124th to 162d St.....	21,330,000	1.95	9.00
St. Nicholas Av., Fort Washington Av., 162d to 175th Street........................	4,900,000	.75	2.20
Ft. Washington Av., 175th to 193d St.	4,615,000	.95	1.90
Total	$159,583,000	16.82	56.66

The following table shows the Board of Transportation's estimated cost of each new route, together with the name of the route and the track mileage:

Route	*Est. Cost*	*Route Miles*	*Track Miles*
Brooklyn Crosstown	$64,884,000	9.24	19.18
Culver Line Extension	60,000,000	5.77	22.44
Bronx-Concourse	38,681,000	4.85	12.20
Houston-Essex and Rutgers Sts.	17,337,000	2.08	6.26
193d-216th Streets	5,144,000	.96	1.92
Total	$186,046,000	22.90	62.00

The Board of Transportation estimates provide for engineering, administration, interest, the cost of real estate, etc., but do not include shops, yards or equipment. The report points out that the most costly items in the estimates' expenditures are the tunnels, three of which will be under the East River, one under the Harlem River, one under Newtown Creek and another under the Gowanus Canal.

The length of routes and estimate of cost of construction is exclusive of lead tracks to yards and shops, land for and construction of yards and shops, and property to be taken in connection with the construction of the routes enumerated.

In connection with its report in December the Board of Transportation supplemented its statistical summary with the information contained in the excerpt from the press which follows:

> The estimated cost of property and easements to be taken for additional Manhattan transit lines is $10,000,000.
>
> Estimated cost of shops and yards is $5,000,000.

It is probable that the cost of easements, inspection and repair shops and storage yards for the track outlined in the second report is as great as that of the first report or $15,000,000.

The above cost and mileage statistical summaries need but little comment. If to the estimated costs of the two separate summaries $30,000,000 is added for easements and necessary facilities, we get the total cost of the system. The estimated cost of the routes, as far as adopted, is $345,629,000. This gives a total of $375,-629,000 for the system as far as outlined exclusive of equipment or an indicated cost of $3,200,000 per single mile of track for the 119 miles outlined.

According to Mr. Ridgway the cost of equipment is in the neighborhood of 40 per cent of that of the cost of construction. But cost of construction per single mile of track varies. Not so with cost of equipment. The cost of the 65 miles announced in December was estimated at $188,000,000 which included $15,000,000 for easements and yard facilities. At the transit hearing conducted by Judge McAvoy, Mr. Ridgway testified that the cost of the mileage as then announced and of the equipment combined would be approximately $254,000,-000. That gives $66,000,000 for equipment alone or about $1,000,000 per single mile of track. It gives us $4,200,000 as the combined cost of constructing and equipping a single mile of track of the independent system as per reports of the Board of Transportation.

In a later report covering the entire system, the estimated cost per single mile of track is given as $3,700,-000. It is the carefully formed judgment of the writer that the proportion of trunk to feeder line tracks that will ultimately be constructed will be increased. As trunk lines cost more to construct than feeder lines, we will use $4,000,000 as the more probable average cost of constructing and equipping the urgently needed new rapid transit lines.

If operating revenue equals or exceeds operating expenses and fixed charges, then the fare charged a passenger covers the cost of carrying him. Let us, therefore, examine operating revenue and operating expenses on existing rapid transit systems to get data for estimating the cost of carrying a passenger on lines constructed, equipped and operated at the prevailing price of material and cost of labor. The table which follows shows operating revenue for a single mile of track:

OPERATING REVENUE, YEAR ENDED JUNE 30, 1924

Company	*Operating Revenue*	*Miles of Single Track*	*Revenue per Mile of Single Track*
I. R. T. Subway	$38,392,635	218	$176,000
I. R. T. Elevated	19,381,140	123	158,000
B. M. T. Rapid Transit	27,652,431	263	105,000

The table which follows mirrors the operating ratio, that is, the per cent of operating revenue that is absorbed by operating expenses:

PERCENT OF OPERATING REVENUE ABSORBED BY OPERATING EXPENSES

Company	*Operating Revenue* 1924	*Operating Expenses* 1924	*Expenses Per Cent of Revenue*
I. R. T. Subway	$38,392,635	$21,956,633	57+
I. R. T. Elevated	19,381,140	11,884,782	62—
B. M. T. Rapid Transit	27,652,431	18,311,991	66+

The above summaries cover only one fiscal year. In order to get a correct perspective, we must have as a background revenue per single mile of track for a series of years. In the following summary we give these additional figures for the period covered by State regulation, that is, for the period beginning with the fiscal year ended June 30, 1908, for the I. R. T. Subway Division.

OPERATING REVENUE PER SINGLE MILE OF TRACK
JUNE 30, 1908 to JUNE 30, 1924

Year	*Miles of Track*	*Operating Revenue*	*Revenue for Mile of Track*
1908	79	$10,020,538	$126,442
1909	82	12,191,000	149,780
1910	82	13,932,506	170,033
1911	85	14,353,206	168,248
1912	85	15,693,908	183,856
1913	85	16,807,956	196,953
1914	85	17,560,558	205,772
1915	88	17,843,795	203,070
1916	88	19,357,253	219,594
1917	137	21,454,893	157,041
1918	142	21,840,448	153,622
1919	199	24,632,208	124,493
1920	204	31,622,973	155,022
1921	212	34,827,415	163,971
1922	212	34,642,843	163,102
1923	214	36,344,258	170,135
1924	218	38,312,635	176,000

These statistical summaries and the testimony of Mr. Ridgway will enable us to estimate the amount of revenue per single mile of track that may be reasonably expected on the new mileage after the traffic in the area served is developed to capacity.

The maximum density of traffic was $219,600 per single mile of track in 1916. At that time, the I. R. T. had one trunk line of four tracks and only two feeder lines of two tracks each—Broadway and Lenox Avenue. Now it has two trunk lines having eight tracks and five feeder lines having ten tracks. That is, its feeder lines have increased faster than its trunk lines. In the new mileage, feeder lines are apparently as great a per cent of the total than in the existing I. R. T. system, long haul traffic will apparently be as great a per cent of the total. Congestion of traffic is now primarily focused in the trunk lines. A system in which trunk line tracks are the same per cent of feeder lines as that of the I. R. T., other factors being equal, will have the same revenue producing capacity. Indications are that the new system will have no advantage in these respects over the existing I. R. T. subway lines. The estimate given in the final report of the Board of Transportation confirms it.

If we turn to the table which shows the per cent of operating revenue absorbed by operating expenses, we note that that of the I. R. T. subway division is 57 per cent of revenue. The greater revenue producing capacity of the new mileage is not accompanied by a corresponding increase in operating expenses. Owing to fuller use of pneumatic control doors on cars, adequate and up-to-date repair and inspection facilities and materially cheaper power if the mercurial process of electric generation is available at that time, 70 per cent of the operating revenues of today will cover the operating expenses, interest on working capital, and adequate provision for depreciation on the new mileage, or approximately $125,000 per single mile of track after traffic is developed to capacity. That given in the report of the Board of Transportation is $150,000 per single mile of track. That is clearly excessive unless the difference, about $25,000 per single mile of track, is approximately the estimated allowance for the inefficiency of the City as an operating agency. Contrast this operating expense figure of the Board of Transportation with that of the I. R. T. subway division $98,000, and elevated division $96,000 per single mile of track in 1924.

We will now assemble the results of our analysis of probable revenue, operating expenses and fixed charges into an income statement so that the indicated loss may stand out more clearly.

ESTIMATED INCOME STATEMENT

Operating Revenues		$225,000
Operating Expenses	$125,000	
Interest & Sinking Fund Charges	200,000	
		325,000
Deficit		$100,000

To get the actual deficit for the projected system it is merely necessary to multiply the $100,000 by the number of miles operated. If the sinking fund is eliminated, the indicated deficit will be reduced $40,000 per single mile of track.

The foregoing observations are predicated on continuance of the existing price level. Since the beginning of the World War, it has been somewhat kaleidoscopic. Hence the deficit shown above merely indicates that subways constructed, equipped and operated at the prevailing price of material and cost of labor as per program of the Board of Transportation cannot be operated at a five-cent fare and cover the cost of carrying a passenger.

The figures given in the above income statements are the indicated deficit or loss after traffic has been developed to capacity. That is about six years after initial operation and probably longer on the extension to Jamaica. During initial operation the deficit will be materially larger becoming progressively smaller until traffic is developed to capacity. It is not necessary to carry this analysis further as the projected system can probably never be translated into a going concern.

We will set over against the foregoing estimated income statement per single mile of track of the writer one compiled from data published by the Board of Transportation for the tenth year. Its density of traffic is approximately that of the I. R. T. subway division for the fiscal year ended June 30, 1924.

BOARD OF TRANSPORTATION INCOME STATEMENT

Revenue		$260,000
Operating Expenses	$150,000	
Interest & Sinking Fund Charges	185,000	
		335,000
Deficit or Loss		$75,000

The cost of carrying a passenger is not an amount that is rigidly fixed but is severely elastic. It depends to an appreciable extent on how costly it is made. If business considerations dominate in the laying out of routes, that is, if trunk and feeder line tracks are provided in proper proportion so that each can be operated to capacity after traffic is developed, five cents will or can be made to cover costs. Rapid transit lines, under existing political conditions, should be planned with reference to making five cents cover the cost of the service and buses should be fostered as feeders and as distributors of rapid transit lines that are themselves feeders and distributors of trunk lines in business centers.

If traffic taxes all sections of a system to capacity, that is, if there are adequate feeders of feeders to trunk lines in and to business centers a passenger can be carried for five cents without excessive discomfort if the amount of long haul traffic is not excessive.

The I. R. T. Queens program was based on this policy. A network of surface lines were to have been developed as feeders of a feeder rapid transit line to trunk lines to and in downtown Manhattan. The program came to grief as a result of the upheaval in the price level due to the world war. It was predicated on correct traffic principles.

Our conclusions on the amount of debt-incurring power needed for the construction of new subways are based on the existing ratio between feeder and trunk line tracks and between long and short haul traffic. It is $225,000 revenue per single mile of track for the I. R. T. subways after the local stations are lengthened so as to accommodate ten car trains.

On the B. M. T. the revenue per single mile of track was $105,000 for the fiscal year ended June 30, 1924. We have already noted that the company claims that it can be doubled, if relatively inexpensive changes in and additions to the existing structures and facilities are made. That forecast includes the elevated lines and operation under existing traffic conditions. From these observations it appears that on the subway and reconstructed lines a density of traffic yielding $225,000 per single mile of track can be accommodated without excessive discomfort after the changes in and additions to the existing facilities have been made.

It is not necessary to go into greater refinements. The amount of revenue that can be derived from a single mile of track is to an appreciable extent a matter of planning. If there is a proper proportion of trunk line to feeder line tracks and if feeder lines are trunk lines of a network of buses which are its feeders and distributors revenue per single mile of track will be higher than the $225,000 per single mile of track that we used in our computations to show the amount of debt-incurring that should be made available for new construction. A sane policy in planning can be fostered if the two per centum to which local taxes are restricted is made to cover the interest and sinking fund charge on subway or revenue producing investments.

We have already noted that the existing rapid transit lines can be made self-sustaining on a five-cent fare under a new legal structure in which all charges to income are eliminated save those that are an actual and necessary part of the cost of carrying a passenger including taxes. New lines if they are scientifically planned as an organic part of existing lines can be made self-sustaining on a five-cent fare, that is, if planned so as to limit the length of the haul and permit utilization of all feeder and trunk line tracks to capacity whether new or old.

We can illustrate the principle developed in the preceding paragraphs by reference to the Manhattan elevated revenue per single mile of track as of June 30, 1924. That revenue was $158,000. It only operates seven car trains during the rush hour period of the day. As per testimony given at the recent transit hearing already referred to, a new car has double the capacity of an old car. In mass transportation it probably has only one and three-fourths the carrying capacity of an old car. The B. M. T. has urged the City to lengthen its station platforms so that they will accommodate eight car trains. That is about the equivalent of a train of fourteen Manhattan elevated cars. Therefore, if on the new lines the same proportion of short haul to long haul traffic and of trunk lines to feeder lines is provided, the revenue per single mile of track may exceed $320,000 per year after traffic has been developed to capacity.

If new subway lines are planned as extensions of existing lines and if the entire system through these extensions is shaped on a model of which the Manhattan elevated serves as a type, and if that system is operated as efficiently as is the subway division of the I. R. T. at present—free from taxes; from the sinking fund charge; and deficits on new lines are charged to taxes until traffic is developed with credit at the low rate of interest of the City—such a system under such a legal structure can be operated at a five-cent fare and cover the actual and necessary cost of carrying a passenger. In short, if items of cost are reduced or eliminated as indicated in this analysis and if new lines are scientifically planned as extensions of existing lines, a passenger can be carried for five cents.

Revenue per single mile of track on the subway division of the I. R. T. may also serve as a basis for computing revenue on new lines after traffic is developed to capacity and, in so doing, confirm the conclusions derived by the use of the revenue per single mile of track on the Manhattan elevated. That revenue was $176,000 for the fiscal year ended June 30, 1924. Its average train length was eight (8) cars. Those of the new system, as announced, will be the equivalent of twelve (12) I. R. T. cars. Other things being equal, the revenue on new lines will be $264,000 per single mile of track or 50 per cent greater—the per cent that its average train length will be greater. The figure derived from data given in the report of the Board of Transportation is $260,000. But the revenue per single mile of track was $220,000 for the fiscal year ended June 30, 1916. During the rush period, eight local and ten express car train were operated or an average of nine car trains. At that time the proportion of trunk lines to feeder lines was 50—50 and not 8—10 as today. If the new lines had the same or 1916 ratio of trunk to feeder line tracks and of short to long haul traffic then because of the 33 1-3 per cent greater train length, the new lines would have a revenue producing capacity of $290,000 per single mile of track, after traffic is developed to capacity and that is virtually enough to cover the actual and necessary cost (sinking fund excluded) of carrying a passenger at the then and at the existing density of traffic.

At present the subway division of the I. R. T. has ten feeder line and eight trunk line tracks for the Manhattan-Queens section. If this ratio were the reverse, that is, if there were ten trunk line and eight feeder line tracks with local stations of ten car train lengths and if there were a system of buses as feeders and distributors of these feeders the system would be self-sustaining if items that are not an actual and necessary part of the cost of carrying a passenger were eliminated.

For Manhattan, The Bronx and Queens, it requires approximately twelve feeder line to sixteen trunk line tracks between 54th Street and Canal Street, Manhattan—all properly located for five cents to cover the cost of carrying a passenger after traffic is developed provided there is a similar extension into Brooklyn with a two-way movement of traffic mornings and evenings through the business section of both boroughs.

On the existing I. R. T. subway system we have the greatest volume of traffic where there are the least number of tracks. It is self-evident that if the feeder lines have greater carrying capacity than the trunk lines that there will be congestion on the trunk lines and a wasteful service on the feeder lines—the trunk lines will not only have the traffic which originates on the feeder lines but also their own short haul traffic. Clearly the carrying capacity of the trunk lines should be greater than that of the feeders by the carrying capacity required by its own short haul traffic, that is, traffic that originates and ends in its own area. The nearer the approach to this ideal or ratio, the lower the cost of carrying a passenger. Traffic to capacity requires a system of buses as feeders and distributors of feeder rapid transit lines. It also requires the fullest development of a two-way movement of traffic in business centers both mornings and evenings. That distributes the fixed charges for the costly business center construction.

Instead of having the neck (lesser number of tracks) so to speak in the middle of the bottle as in the case of the Contract No. 3 operating system or none as in the case of Contract No. 1 and Contract No. 2 subways the neck (lesser number of tracks) should be at both ends and there should be a two-way movement of traffic both mornings and evenings in business centers. Having the neck in the middle of a system as at present means a wasteful service.

The Manhattan elevated is the creation of men of business insight. In the planning of the existing subways business considerations were subordinated to those of a social character—dispersion of the City's population. In the planning of new lines these considerations should be properly blended and initial deficits, until traffic is developed, should be charged to taxes.

The fare that will cover costs depends on length of trains and on the ratio of trunk and feeder lines to each other and even on the extent to which these feeders are served by busses as feeders and distributors. Revenue producing capacity is not determined by the number of miles of track except and in-so-far as feeders produce the volume of traffic that can be carried through the neck of the bottle—vital points in trunk lines to business centers. Feeders beyond that point are uneconomical—wasteful. Of that character is the existing rapid transit line to Queens. Its adoption called for an additional trunk line to lower Manhattan. A unified system will make possible such an increase in the ratio of trunk to feeder line tracks and of short haul to long haul traffic on existing subway and elevated lines through inclusion of extensions that five cents will cover the cost of carrying a passenger if the system is not extended beyond the City limits.

In computing the income statement items used in this chapter the writer started with actual revenue and actual operating expense figures per single mile of track on actual systems. The increase in revenue for up-to-date systems were predicated on the same number of trains operated the same distance but with the length of eight cars of the proposed system. Revenue was increased in the proportion that the train capacity of the proposed system is greater than that of the present. In operating expenses, the estimated figure of the Board of Transportation is used because it is larger than what the writer believes the actual figure will be. Owing to the universal use of multiple-control doors and turnstiles operating expenses will not increase as fast as revenue due to mere increase in train length. Adequate provision for depreciation will materially increase operating expenses but in all probability not from the $98,000 I. R. T. subway division and the $96,000 elevated division figures to the $150,000 estimated figure of the Board of Transportation.

Another feature in rapid transit calls for serious consideration. It was included in the preliminary report of the Board of Transportation on the Eighth Avenue line but excluded in its final or May 26th report. Daniel L. Turner, Consulting Engineer of the Transit Commission and of the Board of Transportation, recommends its adoption in connection with his plan for the supersession of the Third Avenue Elevated by a subway, that is a six-track subway composed of four express and two local tracks. Of it he says:

> Such a six-track subway, four tracks of which are express tracks, would have the same rush hour capacity as two ordinary four-track lines, each with two local and two express tracks.

Mr. Turner estimates that a four-track subway from the City Hall to Harlem River (7.6 route miles) will cost $85,000,000 and that as a six-track subway it will cost only $115,000,000. In short a $115,000,000 investment on the six-track basis gives the same carrying capacity as twice $85,000,000 ($170,000,000) investment on a four-track basis—a saving of $55,000,000 in construction, amounting to approximately a saving of $45,000 in the interest charge per single mile of track.

These observations indicate that six-track subways in streets and avenues in the business centers of Brooklyn and Manhattan having elevated lines should be given serious consideration in the planning of a comprehensive system. It may well be that it is the method that should be employed to secure elimination of the elevated structures from business centers simultaneously with creating a system in which trunk and feeder line tracks bear such a proportion to each other that on it a five-cent fare will be self-sustaining without undue crowding.

The economies that can be effected through planning subways by giving greater weight to business considerations than have been given to it in the last twenty-five years may be summarized as follows:

(a) More intensive use of new and of existing feeder line track thereby materially reducing the interest charge on them per unit of traffic—carrying capacity being increased by mere increase in trunk line track capacity.

(b) Economies through better articulation of the Brooklyn and Manhattan trunk line tracks thereby increasing the two-way movement of traffic on these tracks as that of Brooklyn and Manhattan moves in opposite directions in the morning and in the evening. If the two-way movement of traffic is large, the reduction in interest charge per unit of traffic in the trunk line area may be so substantial that it will approach 50 per cent.

(c) In addition to the economies noted above, there will be a material saving of interest per unit of carrying capacity if six-track trunk line subways are constructed having the equivalent carrying capacity of two four-track subways thereby creating a more perfect proportion of express and local tracks than is possible on four-track subways. Such a subway can be constructed at a reduction of about 32½ per cent in the cost of a unit of carrying capacity which simultaneously reduces the cost of credit on the trunk line track having this type of construction the same per cent.

As long as five cents covered the cost of carrying a passenger business considerations were not of controlling importance in planning new subways, but now that five cents does not cover the actual and necessary cost of carrying a passenger unless all sections of the system are operated to capacity, planning of additional transit facilities is of controlling importance. To the extent that other than business considerations enter into the planning of new rapid transit lines to that extent deficits should be charged to taxes. This analysis shows that under a proper legal structure five cents will cover the *actual and necessary* cost of carrying a passenger on a properly planned rapid transit system.

CHAPTER XVI.

RESUME, MAINTAINING THE FIVE-CENT FARE

We have so far shown that under a legal structure in which only items of expense that are an actual and necessary part of the cost of carrying a passenger are charged to transit income five cents will cover the cost—not in a parlor car but from a place of origin to a to a destination within the City limits without excessive discomfort if the facilities are scientifically located and properly coordinated.

The conditions for preserving the five-cent fare without resort to taxation are as follows:

(1) Station platforms should be lengthened where necessary so that they will accommodate ten car trains on all lines of the I. R. T. subway system and eight car trains on the B. M. T. subways and reconstructed lines.

(2) There should be enough trunk lines in business centers to accommodate their own local traffic and the traffic of its feeders and distributors, that is, there should be more trunk line tracks in business centers

than feeder line tracks to these trunk line tracks when viewed from the standpoint of one way movement of traffic in the morning and the reverse in the evening.

(3) New feeder line tracks should be properly located with reference to existing feeder lines and they themselves should be trunk lines of buses privately owned and operated so that they will serve as feeders and distributors of traffic of feeder rapid transit lines. This would give a semi-commuters service for the sparsely settled outlying districts of the City.

(4) Elimination of the sinking fund as a compulsory charge to transit income. It should be charged to taxes in-so-far as it cannot be abandoned.

(5) Credit for extension of existing facilities should be made available at the low rate of interest that the City enjoys.

(6) Title to all privatèly owned rapid transit facilities and rights should be vested in the City through a municipally owned corporation which should be organized so that it will be a non-political agency for the operation of all rapid transit facilities as a unified system.

(7) Deficits incurred in fostering dispersion of population should be charged to taxes in-so-far as they are not covered by profits on other parts of the system.

(8) Deficits on operation of revenue producing enterprises should be included in the 2 per cent tax limit contained in the constitution so that greater care will be exercised in the selection of new routes.

In this study of the transit situation the writer developed certain guiding principles. These are as follows:

(1) There should be no liberalization of the 10 per cent debt limit provision of the constitution for additional subway construction except as a last resort.

(2) Teeth should be put into the 2 per cent tax limit provision of the constitution by including interest on bonds issued for revenue producing enterprises.

(3) The principle of a self-sustaining fare should be embodied in the constitutional structure of the State but charges to transit income should exclude items that are not an actual and necessary part of the cost of carrying a passenger through modification of the existing constitutional and legal structure upon which transit rests.

(4) The investment of the City under Contract No. 3 and Contract No. 4 should be made self-sustaining without any unnecessary delay.

Not enough debt-incurring power is available for the construction of urgently needed new subways and for the erection of urgently needed new school buildings. Therefore, an agency should be created which can raise the money for equipping new subways at the low rate of interest that the City enjoys and which can acquire the privately owned rapid transit facilities and rights upon reasonable terms for and on behalf of the City, operate them as a non-political agency, and, in so doing, make the entire investment self-sustaining including the existing investment of the City thereby making the debt-incurring power of the City now absorbed under the Dual Contracts available for new construction. A municipally owned corporation empowered to issue municipally guaranteed transit bonds will answer the purpose.

If the constitutional and legal structure is modified so as to eliminate from compulsory charges to transit income the sinking fund and deficits incurred in fostering disperson of population over new lines the companies probably will not offer much opposition to vesting title to their privately owned rapid transit facilities and rights to operate non-recapturable subways into a municipially owned corporation at the actuarial value of their earnings for payment to security holders at a five-cent fare. If acquired on those terms, the investment of the Ctiy under existing contracts will become self-sustaining at a five-cent fare.

Rapid transit trackage is not now inadequate. The trackage is not properly distributed. There is unseemly congestion but only in spots. That is not corrected by an independent system but by inclusion of adequate trunk lines and of balanced extension of trunk and feeder lines thereafter.

The ratio of feeder lines to trunk lines for one way movement of traffic to and through business centers is approximately eight tracks of the former to twelve tracks of the latter. Approximately the same relationship holds for the reverse movement so that there will be a two-way movement of traffic both mornings and evenings through the business section. That would give sixteen feder line to twelve trunk line tracks but the trunk lines would have a two-way movement both mornings and evenings so that twelve trunk line tracks would really be the equivalent of twenty-four as feeder lines can have only a one-way movement of traffic in the morning and the reverse movement in the evening except for a limited crosstown service.

Correlation of new and existing trunk and feeder lines can be given the fullest expression through a single rapid transit system and not through construction of an independent system. It will permit inclusion of extensions in the existing system that will correct the present unbalanced proportion of trunk and feeder lines.

When the Dual Contracts were negotiated it was the accepted theory of its negotiators that there should be enough trunk lines to carry their own local traffic and that of the feeder lines from outlying territory. If on such a system five cents did not cover the cost of carrying a passenger under the then legal structure the deficit should be paid out of taxes. That conception of transit was made operative through the preferential system of revenue distribution. It was upset by the upheaval in the price level caused by forces set in motion by the world war, and by the refusal of the present city administration to assent to altering the financial clauses of these contracts so as to realize the intent of the negotiators. As a substitute for the principle underlying the Dual Contracts, the City now proposes wholesale taxes and assessment of real estate benefitted. That is merely the principle underlying the Dual Contracts under a different operative method. To this method of giving expression to the principle the opposition is formidable. As a substitute for the principle the writer proposes operation at cost through a non-political agency of a unified rapid transit system, exclusion of deficits due to fostering dispersion of the City's population and of the sinking fund to amortize transit investments from compulsory charges to transit income. Both are inherently fiscal charges and should be charged to taxes. This done, if feeder and trunk lines are properly correlated five cents will cover the cost of carrying a passenger with only such a degree of discomfort as the bulk of the passengers would elect to continue rather than pay for greater comfort through a higher fare. If feeder lines are excessive the deficit will be due to intent to foster dispersion of population and so it will be fiscal in character and a proper charge to taxes. If such deficits are included in the 2 per cent tax limit, excessive construction of feeder lines by the use of municipal credit will be made impossible. It substitutes a principle that operates automatically for that underlying the Dual Contracts which does not work under existing political conditions and similarly will not work under the new method of giving it expression proposed by the Board of Transportation.

The business items of present-day transit expense

should be separated from those of a social character and to the extent that the latter are not covered by transit income at a five-cent fare on new lines or on a unified system to that extent they should be a charge to taxes. Expenses that are of a business character should be borne by the passengers. Those of a social character should be charged to taxes if they are not covered by income derived from a five-cent fare.

All items of expense that are now charged to transit income that are not an actual and necessary part of the cost of carrying a passenger should be eliminated through modification of the legal structure on which transit rests. If under such a legal structure, five cents will cover the actual and necessary cost of carrying a passenger its abandonment would be a political crime. In this study of transit we have shown that under such a legal structure, five cents will cover the actual and necessary cost of carrying a passenger under conditions that the great mass of users would elect rather than have greater comforts at a higher fare.

In the Dual Contracts the taxpayer was placed behind the farepayer to maintain the five-cent fare. It can be maintained intact without any transit burden being placed on the taxpayer if new lines are scientifically articulated with existing lines and if expenses that are not an actual and necessary part of the cost of carrying a passenger are either eliminated or shifted to taxes where they belong.

As heretofore noted, a five-cent fare is a political

necessity. To the City, a self-sustaining fare is a financial necessity. A five-cent fare can be made self-sustaining by creating a unified rapid transit system in which trunk and feeder line track are so correlated that there will be a minimum of idleness of track and waste in the movement of rolling stock, and which, in addition thereto, is free from charges that it is not actually necessary to incur to carry passengers. This can be most equitably effected through supersession of the existing contracts as outlined in this analysis and modification of the legal structure on which transit rests so that the sinking fund and expenditures to foster dispersion of the City's population will be excluded from charges to transit income.

Supersession of these contracts can be most equitably effected through acquisition of the privately owned rapid transit facilities and rights of the companies by the Board of Transportation for and in behalf of the City and leasing them to a municipally owned corporation organized as a nonpolitical agency to operate them in conjunction with new lines as a unified system.

The municipally owned corporation should be vested with authority to issue municipally guaranteed self-sustaining transit bonds in exchange for the transit facilities and rights noted above and for equipping new lines constructed with municipal credit.

Under the unified rapid transit system, charges to transit income under the existing legal structure on which transit rests that are not an actual and necessary part of the cost of carrying a passenger should be excluded. These are:

(a) The sinking fund.

(b) Expenditures to foster dispersion of the City's population.

In computations to determine whether a five-cent fare is self-sustaining as required if this program is adopted provision for a sinking fund and expenditures to foster dispersion of the City's population will be excluded.

Provision should be made so that exclusion of the sinking fund as a charge to transit income will not make inoperative the revolving fund principle in the constitution relative to exemption of self-sustaining subway bonds from the debt limit.

In this analysis of the transit situation, the writer aimed to develop principles which would guide officials in the selection of routes. These principles can be most effectively applied in a unified, five-borough rapid transit system. The paragraph which follows will serve as an illustration.

If in addition to the subways planned for immediate construction by the Transit Commission there are included a six-track subway on Sixth Avenue and on Third Avenue (elevated structures to be removed) properly articulated with existing feeder lines, including a new feeder line to Queens and a tunnel to Staten

Island, the net cost to construct and equip will be approximately that of the independent system proposed by the Board of Transportation. It will, however, increase the carrying capacity of the consolidated system more than three times the estimated carrying capacity of the independent system as projected. As a result, the interest charge per unit of additional carrying capacity will be only about one-third that on the independent system.

This mirrors in a forceful way what can be accomplished through planning if adequate weight is given to business considerations.

This analysis points to the conclusion that you cannot have a subway at everybody's door at a five-cent fare but that you can have rapid transit facilities wherever properly coordinated trunk and feeder lines can be operated to capacity after traffic is developed provided they are not burdened with charges that are fiscal in character, that is, are burdened only with charges that it is necessary to incur to carry passengers as a business enterprise.

www.ingramcontent.com/pod-product-compliance
Lightning Source LLC
LaVergne TN
LVHW021358110826
845150LV00007B/1705

* 9 7 8 1 4 2 5 5 1 3 2 6 9 *